New Revised

A Gift for

Ramadhān

Shaykh Abdul Raheem Limbada
hafizahullāh

Tafseer Raheemi Publications 2021
info@tafseer-raheemi.com

A Gift for Ramadhān
2nd Revised Edition 2nd Print: Ramadhan 1442/April 2021
ISBN: 978-1-912301-08-9

Author & Editing	*Shaykh* Abdul Raheem Limbādā *Hafizahullāh* (www.tafseer-raheemi.com)
Cover Design	Ahmed Bhula
Typesetting	B.I
Printed by	Elma Basim, Istanbul, Turkey (elmabasim.com)

Other available titles in this series:

A Gift for Nikāh

Available to purchase from www.tafseer-raheemi.com/shop

CONTENTS

FOREWORD

IN THE NAME OF ALLĀH ﷻ, the Most Merciful, the Most Kind. All praise is due to Allāh ﷻ who, through His infinite mercy has once again granted us another blessed Month of Ramadhān. May Allāh ﷻ accept and be pleased with us.

Alhamdulillāh, you have before you a very valuable piece of work. A detailed guide to the masā'il of Ramadhān.

Throughout the years, our honourable and respected Shaykh Abdul Raheem [Hafizahullāh] has benefitted countless people in the field of Hadīth, Tafsīr, Tasawwuf and Fiqh through lectures, courses, books and Shaykh's website www.tafseer-raheemi.com.

It was during a course in which Shaykh was teaching his compilation of 40 Hadīth relating to Ramadhān, and it was after teaching this when Shaykh decided to write a book that would act as a complete guide to Ramadhān [spiritually and practically] for one and all.

After spending many hours with Ulama and medical doctors, you have before you a priceless book, which, Inshā-Allāh, will solve many important issues that are faced during the blessed month of Ramadhān for people young and old, in all communities across the globe.

May Allāh ﷻ accept this work and reward Shaykh Abdul Raheem [Hafizahullāh] immensely for his efforts. May Allāh ﷻ also reward the respected Muftī Shabbīr Sahib, Muftī Sūfī Tāhir Saheb, Doctor Mazharuddin Sahib, Doctor Salīm, Doctor Liāqat and Maulānā Zayd Mehtar for their contributions to this valuable piece. May Allāh ﷻ reward Sister Naielah Ackbarali for her well researched and detailed article on Fasting [presented later in the book].

May Allāh ﷻ guide us and protect us all. Āmīn

Ahmed Bhula
General Manager of www.tafseer-raheemi.com
Ramadhān 1436 AH

INTRODUCTION

Allāh ﷻ has introduced the month of Ramadhān in the Holy Qur'ān with the following verse:

شَهْرُ رَمَضَانَ الَّذِيَ اُنْزِلَ فِيْهِ الْقُرْاٰنُ هُدًى لِّلنَّاسِ وَبَيِّنٰتٍ مِّنَ الْهُدٰى وَالْفُرْقَانِ ۚ فَمَنْ شَهِدَ مِنْكُمُ الشَّهْرَ فَلْيَصُمْهُ ۗ وَمَنْ كَانَ مَرِيْضًا اَوْ عَلٰى سَفَرٍ فَعِدَّةٌ مِّنْ اَيَّامٍ اُخَرَ ۗ يُرِيْدُ اللّٰهُ بِكُمُ الْيُسْرَ وَلَا يُرِيْدُ بِكُمُ الْعُسْرَ ۫ وَلِتُكْمِلُوا الْعِدَّةَ وَلِتُكَبِّرُوا اللّٰهَ عَلٰى مَا هَدٰىكُمْ وَلَعَلَّكُمْ تَشْكُرُوْنَ ۞

"The month of Ramadhān is the month in which the Qur'ān was revealed as a guidance for mankind, whose verses of guidance are absolutely clear, and a criterion. So whoever among you witnesses this month, should fast in it. While those who are ill or on a journey should make up for the same number of days at another time. Allāh wants ease for you and does not want hardship for you. You should complete the period and then glorify Allāh that He guided you. And you will perhaps show gratitude to Him." [1]

The verse indicates towards the greatness of this month by saying that the greatest of all divine scriptures, the glorious Qur'ān, was revealed in this blessed month.

This revelation is of two types:

[1] Revelation from Lawhe Mahfooz to the earthly heaven took place in this month in the night of power.

[2] The beginning of revelation upon the heart of the Prophet ﷺ. The first five verses of Sūrah Alaq were revealed in the cave of Hira, in Laylatul Qadr, in this month.

---

[1] Qur'ān 2:185.

14

The Qur'ān came like a heavy rainfall in a hot climate with extreme drought. The world was dry, filled with Kufr, Shirk and disobedience. The Qur'ān came like a heavy rainfall which cools everything down and breathes life into dry lands. It had everything that was needed; guidance, clear proofs, the power to distinguish between truth and false. It breathed life into dead souls.

Since this month holds great virtues, people should fast in it. This fasting is only from dawn till dusk, and only for one month. We can eat and drink freely for eleven months, but we should bring our desires under control for just one month. There is flexibility for the sick and the travellers. This is because Allāh ﷻ is extremely kind and merciful. He does not like putting his creation in difficulties, so he granted flexibility. Allāh ﷻ wants us to complete this period and be grateful to Him for guiding us towards that which benefits us.

People should be grateful and keep fasts properly. We see that in this day and age people miss fasts or break them for silly excuses. There is an environment of godlessness out there. No wonder we suffer from individual misfortunes and collective problems around the world. May Allāh ﷻ guide us.

Some people say summer fasts are too long. However, they fail to realise that the extra effort will bring extra reward and on top of that, the pleasure of Allāh ﷻ, which is our aim.

Rasūlullāh ﷺ would sometimes fast while travelling through the desert, enduring the heat and thirst. The Sahāba ﷺ loved fasting in the hot summer days. They literally felt *lazzat* in their hardship. That is the inner pleasure, the pleasure of the soul and mind, which we so much crave.

Our *salaf* used to love it also. Maulānā Arshad Madani Saheb mentioned that his father Hadhrat Maulānā Hussain Ahmed Madani ﷺ would be fasting in the hot summer days. He would be reciting the Qur'ān to someone after Asr Salāh. His tongue would get stuck and he would struggle to continue. He would get up and go to the *Wudhū* area, pour two jugs of water over his head and come back and continue reading. There was no air conditioning nor any fans in those days.

This book which you have in your hands was written with the intention to make *masā'il* of *Sawm* easy for everyone. We compiled *40 Hadīth* at the beginning, in order to give some encouragement to the readers. Maybe if one person observes fasts properly, this can be a source of salvation for myself and for all our Tafseer Raheemi team. This has been a collective effort rather than an individual one.

I would like to express my gratitude to Allāh 🕊 for giving me the tawfeeq to compile this book, and then I would like to thank the authors of the books I have benefited from, mainly *'Tuhfae Ramadhān'* by Muftī Salmān Mansūrpūrī. I should also mention and thank my dearest Muftī Zaid Mehtar who was the main driving force behind this. And then our Tafseer Raheemi manager Ahmed Bhula. Also Yahya Batha, Esa Bhai and the rest of the team.

May Allāh 🕊 reward each and every one of them with the best of rewards in *Dunya* and *Akhirah*. Āmīn

Shaykh Abdul Raheem Limbādā *Hafizahullāh*
9 Sha'bān 1437 / 16 May 2016

40 HADĪTH

[1] RASŪLULLĀH ﷺ PAYING GREAT IMPORTANCE TO RAMADHĀN

عن سلمان الفارسي، قال: خطبنا رسول الله صلى الله عليه وسلم في آخر يوم من شعبان فقال أيها الناس قد أظلكم شهر عظيم شهر مبارك شهر فيه ليلة خير من ألف شهر جعل الله صيامه فريضة وقيام ليله تطوعا من تقرب فيه بخصلة من الخير كان كمن أدى فريضة فيما سواه ومن أدى فيه فريضة كان كمن أدى سبعين فريضة فيما سواه وهو شهر الصبر والصبر ثوابه الجنة وشهر المواساة وشهر يزداد فيه رزق المؤمن من فطر فيه صائما كان مغفرة لذنوبه وعتق رقبته من النار وكان له مثل أجره من غير ان ينتقص من أجره شيء قالوا ليس كلنا نجد ما يفطر الصائم فقال يعطي الله هذا الثواب من فطر صائما على تمرة أو شربة ماء أو مذقة لبن وهو شهر أوله رحمة واوسطه مغفرة وآخره عتق من النار من خفف عن مملوكه غفر الله له واعتقه من النار واستكثروا فيه من أربع خصال خصلتين ترضون بهما ربكم وخصلتين لا غنى بكم عنها فأما الخصلتان اللتان ترضون بهما ربكم فشهادة أن لا إله إلا الله وتستغفرونه وأما اللتان لاغنى بكم عنها فتسألون الله الجنة وتعوذون به من النار ومن أشبع فيه صائما سقاه الله من حوضي شربة لا يظمأ حتى يدخل الجنة ». رواه ابن خزيمة في صحيحه ـ

Hadhrat Salmān ﷺ reports "On the last day of Sha'bān, Allāh's Messenger ﷺ addressed us and said: 'O people, there comes over you now a great month, a most blessed month in which lies a night more greater in virtue than one thousand months. It is a month in which Allāh (The Glorified and the Exalted) has made compulsory that the days should be observed by fasting. And he has made optional the standing by night. Whosoever makes an attempt to draw nearer to Allāh ﷺ by performing any virtuous deed, for him shall be the reward like one who had performed fardh at any other time. And whoever performs fardh, for him shall be the reward of seventy fardh in any other time. This is indeed the month of patience, and the reward for true patience is Paradise. It is the month of sympathy with one's fellowmen. It is the month wherein a true believer's rizq (sustenance) is increased. Whosoever feeds another who fasted, in order to break the fast (at sunset), for him shall be forgiveness for his sins and emancipation from the fire of Hell and for him shall be the same reward as for him (who he fed) without that person's reward being decreased in the least.

Thereupon we said: "O Messenger of Allāh, not all of us possess the means whereby we can help a fasting person to break his fast." The Messenger of Allāh replied: 'Allāh grants the same reward to him who gives a fasting person, to break the fast, a mere date or a drink of water or a sip of milk. This is a month, the first part of which brings Allāh's Mercy, the middle of which brings His forgiveness and the last of which brings emancipation from the fire of Hell. Whosoever lessens the burden of His servants (labourers) in this month, Allāh (The Glorified and the Exalted) will forgive him and free him from the fire of Hell. And in this month, four things you should continue to perform in great number, two of which shall be to please your Rabb while the other two shall be those without which you cannot do. Those which shall be to please your Rabb, are that you should, abundantly, bear witness that there is no deity to worship except Allāh (i.e. recite the Kalima Tayyibah: La Ilaaha Illallah abundantly) and make much Istighfār (beg Allāh's forgiveness with Astaghfirullāh). And as for those without which you cannot do, you should beg of Allāh entrance into

Paradise and seek refuge in Him from Hell." And whoever satiated a person with food, Allāh (The Glorified and the Exalted) will give him water from the Hawdh (pond) where after he shall never again feel thirsty until he enters Paradise." [2]

[2] FASTING IS A PILLAR OF ISLAM

قال رسول الله صلى الله عليه وسلم بني الإسلام على خمس : شهادة أن لا إله إلا الله وأن محمدا رسول الله ، واقام الصلاة ، وايتاء الزكاة ، والحج ، وصوم رمضان. اخرجه البخاري ـ

"Islam is based on five pillars: To bear witness that there is none worthy of worship except Allāh and that Muhammad is Allāh's Messenger, to establish Salāh, to give Zakāh, to perform Hajj and to Fast in Ramadhān." [3]

[3] RAMADHAN EXPIATES SINS

عن أبي هريرة أن رسول الله صلى الله عليه وسلم كان يقول الصلوات الخمس والجمعة إلى الجمعة ورمضان إلى رمضان مكفرات ما بينهن إذا اجتنب الكبائر رواه مسلم ـ

Abū Hurairah ⿻ narrates that Rasūlullāh ⿻ said, "The five daily prayers, and one Jumu'ah to another Jumu'ah, and one Ramadhān to another Ramadhān, expiate the sins in between as long as one refrains from major sins." [4]

---

[2] Ibn Khuzaimah.
[3] Bukhārī.
[4] Muslim.

[4] IN RAMADHAN, THE GATES OF JANNAH ARE OPENED AND THE GATES OF JAHANNAM ARE CLOSED

عن أبي هريرة رضي الله عنه أن رسول الله صلى الله عليه وسلم قال: إذا جاء رمضان فُتّحت أبواب الجنة، وغُلّقت أبواب النار، وصُفّدت الشياطين. رواه مسلم ـ

Abū Hurairah ﷺ narrates that Rasūlullāh ﷺ said, "When the month of Ramadhān commences, the doors of the heavens are opened, the doors of Jahannam are closed, and the Shayateen are chained." [5]

This results in lessening of sins due to the reasons of sins being minimized. When the gates of Jannah are opened, it's cool breeze reaches the hearts of the believers and urges them to increase their devotion.

[5] FASTING SHOULD BE WITH BELIEF AND SINCERITY

عن أبي هريرة رضي الله عنه قال: قال رسول الله صلى الله عليه وسلم: من صام رمضان إيماناً واحتساباً، غُفر له ما تقدم من ذنبه. رواه الشيخان ـ

Abu Hurairah ﷺ narrates that Rasūlullāh ﷺ said "Whosoever fast in Ramadhān with firm belief and with hope of gaining reward (sincerity), his previous sins will be forgiven." [6]

---

[5] Muslim.
[6] Bukhārī, Muslim.

[6] FIVE GREAT GIFTS FOR A SAAIM

عن أبي هريرة قال قال رسول الله صلى الله عليه وسلم : أعطيت أمتي خمس خصال في رمضان لم تعطها أمة قبلهم خلوف فم الصائم أطيب عند الله من ريح المسك وتستغفر لهم الملائكة حتى يفطروا ويزين الله عز وجل كل يوم جنته ثم يقول يوشك عبادي الصالحون ان يلقوا عنهم المؤنة والأذى ويصيروا إليك ويصفد فيه مردة الشياطين فلا يخلصوا إلى ما كانوا يخلصون إليه في غيره ويغفر لهم في آخر ليلة قيل يا رسول الله أهي ليلة القدر قال لا ولكن العامل إنما يوفى أجره إذا قضى عمله. رواه احمد ـ

Abu Hurairah ﷺ relates that Rasūlullāh ﷺ said, "My Ummah has been given five things for Ramadhān which were not given to anyone except them. For them:

[1] The khuloof of a saaim (smell exiting from the mouth due to emptiness of the stomach) is sweeter to Allāh ﷺ than the fragrant smell of musk. (i.e. Allāh ﷺ loves the saaim due to his sacrifice).

[2] The fishes of the oceans seek forgiveness for the fasting person until they break their fast. [Due to their love for the Saaimeen].

[3] Allāh ﷺ decorates Jannah every day and then says, "The time is near when My faithful servants shall cast aside the great trials of the world and come to you."

[4] In this month the rebellious, giant Satans are chained so that they cannot reach unto those evils to which they normally reached during other months besides Ramadhān.

[5] On the last night of Ramadhān people are forgiven". The Sahābāh ﷺ thereupon enquired, "0 Messenger of Allāh, is that last night Laylatul Qadr? Rasūlullāh ﷺ replied, "No. But a labourer is paid his wage in full, when he completes the work. " [7]

[7] THE REWARD OF SAWM
WILL BE BEYOND IMAGINATION

عن أبي هريرة رضي الله عنه عن النبي صلى الله عليه وسلم قال : « كل عمل ابن آدم يضاعف، الحسنة عشرة أمثالها إلى سبعمائة ضعف قال الله عز وجل : إلا الصوم فإنه لي وأنا أجزي به، يدع شهوته وطعامه من أجلي، للصائم فرحتان:فرحة عند فطره وفرحة عند لقاء ربه، ولخلوف فيه أطيب عند الله من ريح المسك » رواه مسلم ـ

Abu Hurairah ﷺ relates that Rasūlullāh ﷺ said, "Every deed of the son of Ādam, brings 10 hasanāt/rewards and it can be increased up to 700.

(However), Allāh says, 'Except for fast, because fasting is for Me, and I shall reward it. The Saaim leaves his desires and food for My sake.' For a fasting person there are two joys:

[1] A joy at the time of Iftaar.

[2] And a joy when he meets his Lord. The khuloof of a fasting person is more beloved to Allāh than the fragrance of musk. [8]

---

[7] Ahmed.
[8] Muslim.

This means that the rewards of general deeds will be distributed, through the angels. However, fasting is so beloved to Allāh ﷻ, that He himself will personally give its reward. When Allāh ﷻ is generous and he has no fear of poverty, imagine how much He will give.

[8] ABUNDANCE OF RAHMAH FOR THE SAAIMEEN

عن عبادة بن صامت قال قال رسول الله صلى الله عليه و سلم أتاكم رمضان

شهر بركة يغشاكم الله فيه فينزل الرحمة ويحط الخطايا ويستجيب فيه الدعاء

وينظر الله تعالى الى تنافسكم ويباهي بكم ملائكته فأروا الله تعالى من أنفسكم

خيرا فإن الشقي من حرم فيه رحمة الله عزوجل رواه ـ

Ubādah bin Sāmit ﷺ relates that Rasūlullāh ﷺ said "Ramadhān, the month of blessings has come upon you, wherein Allāh turns towards you and sends down His special mercy, He forgives your sins and accepts duās. He observes you're competing with one another in doing good deeds and He boasts to the angels about you. So show to Allāh your righteousness for verily, the most pitiable and unfortunate one is he who is deprived of Allāh's mercy, even in this month.

[9] DUĀS OF A SAAIM ARE ACCEPTED

عن ابي هريرة قال قال رسول الله صلى الله عليه و سلم ثلاثة لا ترد دعوتهم :

الصائم حتى يفطر ، والإمام العادل ، ودعوة المظلوم يرفعها الله فوق الغمام ،

ويفتح لها أبواب السماء ويقول الرب : وعزتي لأنصرنك ولو بعد حين. رواه

الترمذي ـ

Abu Hurairah ﷺ relates that Rasūlullāh ﷺ said: "Three types of people whose supplications are not rejected:

[1] A Fasting person when he opens his fast.

[2] A just ruler.

[3] Duā of a person who is oppressed. Allāh lifts it up to the heavens and the doors of heaven are opened and Allāh says "By My honour! I will indeed help you even though it could be after a while." [9]

[10] TAWFEEQ OF KHAYR IN RAMADHĀN

عَنْ أَبِيْ هُرَيْرَةَ قَالَ : قَالَ رَسُوْلُ الله صَلَّى اللهُ عَلَيْهِ وَسَلَّمَ : " إِذَا كَانَ أَوَّلُ لَيْلَةٍ مِنْ شَهْرِ رَمَضَانَ صُفِّدَتِ الشَّيَاطِيْنُ، وَمَرَدَةُ الْجِنِّ، وَغُلِّقَتْ أَبْوَابُ النَّارِ، فَلَمْ يُفْتَحْ مِنْهَا بَابٌ، وَفُتِّحَتْ أَبْوَابُ الْجَنَّةِ، فَلَمْ يُغْلَقْ مِنْهَا بَابٌ، وَيُنَادِيْ مُنَادٍ : يَا بَاغِيَ الْخَيْرِ أَقْبِلْ، وَيَا بَاغِيَ الشَّرِّ أَقْصِرْ، وَلِلّٰهِ عُتَقَاءُ مِنَ النَّارِ، وَذٰلِكَ كُلَّ لَيْلَةٍ ـ

When it is the first night of Ramadhān, the Satans and the rogue Jinns are chained. The doors of Jahannam are locked, none of them are opened. The doors of Jannah are opened, none of them are closed. And an announcer announces: "O seeker of good! Proceed! And O seeker of evil! Stop!" And Allāh emancipates people from the fire, and this takes place every night." [10]

The whole Hadīth explains that the Tawfeeq of Khayr (the ability to do good deeds) is increased in Ramadhān, whereas the channels of evil are reduced during this holy month.

---

[9] Tirmīdhī.
[10] Tirmīdhī, Ibn Mājah, Mishkāt Pg.173.

[11] NIGHT PRAYER OF RAMADHĀN BRINGS FORGIVENESS

عن أبي هريرة رضي الله عنه أن رسول الله صلى الله عليه وسلم قال:

من قام رمضان إيماناً واحتساباً غُفر له ما تقدم من ذنبه متفق عليه ـ

Abū Hurairah ؓ narrates that Rasūlullāh ﷺ said: "Whosoever stands (in prayer) in Ramadhān with firm belief and with hope of gaining reward, his previous sins will be forgiven." [11]

The indication is towards Tarāwīh Salāh. One should perform it with utmost willingness, show some desire.

[12] STANDING FOR SALAH IN LAYLATUL QADR ATTRACTS FORGIVENESS

عن أبي هريرة رضي الله عنه عن النبي صلى الله عليه وسلم قال:

من قام ليلة القدر إيماناً واحتساباً ، غُفر له ما تقدم من ذنبه متفق عليه ـ

Abū Hurairah ؓ narrates that Rasūlullāh ﷺ said "Whosoever stands (for worship) in Laylatul Qadr (the night of power) with firm belief and with hope of gaining reward, his previous sins will be forgiven." [12]

Note: Laylatul Qadr can be any night from the last 10 nights, most likely one of the odd ones. (21st, 23rd, 25th, 27th and 29th). One should try and stay awake on these nights and perform some kind of worship.

---

[11] Bukhārī, Muslim.
[12] Bukhārī, Muslim.

[13] FASTING EXPIATES SINS

عن حذيفة بن اليمان رضي الله عنه قال: قال رسول الله صلى الله عليه وسلم:
فتنة الرجل في أهله وماله وولده وجاره، تكفّرها الصلاة، والصوم، والصدقة،
والأمر والنهي متفق عليه ـ

Huzaifah ﷺ narrates that Rasūlullāh ﷺ said: "The tests a man faces in his
family, wealth, children and neighbours are expiated by Salāh, Sawm,
Sadaqah and by calling towards good and forbidding from evil." [13]

Note: These tests can be the minor sins committed due to pressure from
family and children, or due to earning and spending wealth without due care,
or due to some differences with one's neighbours. Since they are not major
things, they can be pardoned due to fasting and the good deeds mentioned.

[14] NOTHING CAN MATCH SAWM

عن أبي أمامة رضي الله عنه قال: أتيت رسول الله صلى الله عليه وسلم فقلت:
مرني بأمر آخذه عنك، فقال: عليك بالصوم، فإنه لا مثل له. رواه النسائي ـ

"Abu Umāmah ﷺ says: I came to Rasūlullāh ﷺ and requested him to give
me some advice to which I can hold on. He replied: "Hold on to Sawm,
because it has no similitude." [14]

Note: Fasting is a special act of worship. One Hadīth says: "Everything has a
door, and the door of worship is fasting." The author of Hidāyah wrote the
book in eleven [11] years. He wrote the book whilst fasting all the time, and
in such a way that not even his family knew that he was fasting. He would

---

[13] Bukhārī, Muslim.
[14] Nasa'ī.

take a tiffin from home and return with it empty. He would call some poor person in the afternoon and feed it to him.

[15] SAWM PROTECTS FROM THE FIRE

عن عثمان بن عفان رضي الله عنه، قال: سمعت رسول الله صلى الله عليه
وسلم يقول: الصيام جُنّة من النار، كجنّة أحدكم من القتال. رواه ابن ماجه ـ

Uthmān ﷺ says I heard Rasūlullāh ﷺ saying: "Fasting is a protective shield from the fire, just like one of you has a shield to protect him in the battle."
[15]

[16] AR–RAYYAAN; A SPECIAL GATE OF JANNAH FOR SAAIMEEN

عن سهل بن سعد رضي الله عنه أن النبي صلى الله عليه وسلم قال: في الجنّة
ثمانية أبواب، فيها باب يُسمى الريّان، لا يدخله إلا الصائمون. رواه البخاري،
وزاد النسائي: فإذا دخل آخرهم أغُلق، من دخل فيه شرب، ومن شرب لم
يظمأ أبداً ـ

Sahl bin Saʿd ﷺ narrates that Rasūlullāh ﷺ said: "In Jannah there is a gate called Ar-Rayyān, only the Sā'imūn (people of fasting) will enter it. [16] And in the narration of Nasa'ī there is an addition: When the last person enters, it will be closed, whosoever enters from it, will be given a drink and whomsoever drinks it, will never be thirsty again.

---

[15] Ibn Mājah.
[16] Bukhārī.

Note: Sā'imūn here means those who loved fasting and who used to keep a lot of voluntary fasts.

[17] BEING INVITED FROM ALL GATES

عن أبي هريرة رضي الله عنه أن رسول الله صلى الله عليه وسلم قال من أنفق
زوجين في سبيل الله نودي من أبواب الجنة يا عبد الله هذا خير فمن كان من
أهل الصلاة دعي من باب الصلاة ومن كان من أهل الجهاد دعي من باب
الجهاد ومن كان من أهل الصيام دعي من باب الريان ومن كان من أهل
الصدقة دعي من باب الصدقة فقال أبو بكر رضي الله عنه بأبي أنت وأمي يا
رسول الله ما على من دعي من تلك الأبواب من ضرورة فهل يدعى أحد من
تلك الأبواب كلها قال نعم وأرجو أن تكون منهم رواه البخاري ـ

Abū Hurairah ﷺ narrates that Rasūlullāh ﷺ said: "Whoever spends a pair (of clothes, shoes, or is charitable to double people etc), in the cause of Allāh will be called from the gates of Jannah: "O Abdullāh, this gate is good for you." The people of Salāh will be called from the gate of Salāh, the people of Jihād will be called from the gate of Jihād, the people of Sadaqah will be called from the gate of Sadaqah, and the people of fasting will be called from the gate of Rayyān."

Abu Bakr ﷺ said, "There is no harm on one who will be called from all these gates. So will there be anyone who would be called from all gates?" The Messenger of Allāh ﷺ said, "Yes, and I have great hope that you will be one of them." [17]

---

[17]Bukhārī.

Note: This is because Siddique Akbar ﷺ used to perform all these acts of worship, so he will be called from all the gates. One Hadīth states that Rasūlullāh ﷺ asked a gathering of companions: "Who is fasting today?" Abū Bakr raised his finger. He asked: "Who fed a destitute today?" Abū Bakr raised his finger to say: "I did." He asked: "Who visited a sick person today?" Abū Bakr raised his finger. He asked: "Who attended a funeral today?" Abū Bakr raised his finger. He ﷺ said: "Never do these gather in a person but he will definitely enter Jannah."

It is possible that Rasūlullāh ﷺ had a presentiment [Kashf] in which he realised that Siddique Akbar ﷺ had performed these acts of virtue. He wanted to inform the congregation of the greatness of Siddique Akbar ﷺ so he ﷺ asked these questions.

[18] SPECIAL SEE THROUGH MANSIONS IN JANNAH FOR PEOPLE WHO HAVE FOUR QUALITIES; ONE OF THEM IS SIYAAM

عن علي بن أبي طالب رضي الله عنه قال: قال رسول الله صلى الله عليه وسلم: إن في الجنة غرفاً تُرى ظهورها من بطونها، وبطونها من ظهورها فقام أعرابي فقال: لمن هي يا رسول الله؟ قال: لمن أطاب الكلام، وأطعم الطعام، وأدام الصيام، وصلى لله بالليل والناس نيام رواه الترمذي ـ

Alī bin Abī Tālib ﷺ narrates that Rasūlullāh ﷺ said: "In Paradise there are such rooms that their interior can be seen from outside and outside can be seen from inside. Allāh has prepared them for those who soften their speech, feed people, continuously observe fasts, and perform Salāh at night while people are asleep. [18]

---

[18] Tirmīdhī.

[19] INTERCESSION OF QUR'ĀN AND SIYAAM

عن عبد الله بن عمرو رضي الله عنه أن رسول الله صلى الله عليه وسلم قال:
الصيام والقرآن يشفعان للعبد يوم القيامة، يقول الصيام: أي رب، منعته
الطعام والشهوات بالنهار، فشفعني فيه، ويقول القرآن: منعته النوم بالليل،

فشفعني فيه، فيشفعان رواه أحمد ـ

Abdullāh bin Amr ﷺ narrates that Rasūlullāh ﷺ said: "The fast and Qur'ān
will intercede on behalf of the slave, on the Day of Judgement. The fast will
say: "Yā Rabb! I prevented him from eating, drinking, and fulfilling his
lawful desires during the day, therefore accept my intercession. Qur'ān will
say: Yā Rabb! I prevented him from sleeping at night. So accept my
intercession. Both the intercessions will be accepted." [19]

Note: No one will be allowed to speak up for anyone on the day of Qiyāmah
except with Allāh's permission. So if someone comes forward and puts in a
word for us, imagine how much happiness this will bring us.

[20] EATING SUHOOR UP TO SUBHE SADIQ

عن سهل بن سعد، قال أنزلت {وكلوا واشربوا حتى يتبين لكم الخيط الأبيض
من الخيط الأسود }ولم ينزل من الفجر، فكان رجال إذا أرادوا الصوم ربط
أحدهم في رجله الخيط الأبيض والخيط الأسود، ولم يزل يأكل حتى يتبين له
رؤيتهما، فأنزل الله بعد {من الفجر} فعلموا أنه إنما يعني الليل والنهار رواه
البخاري ـ

---

[19] Ahmed.

Sahl bin Saʻd ﷺ narrates: When the following verses were revealed: 'Eat and drink until the white thread appears to you distinctly from the black thread', and من الفجر (from the dawn) was not yet revealed, some people who intended to fast, tied black and white threads to their feet and went on eating until (there was enough light that) they differentiated between the two. Allāh then revealed the words, 'of dawn', and it became clear that He meant night and day." [20]

i.e Suhoor should be finished by Subhe Sādiq. One cannot eat after that.

Subhe Sādiq means 'True Dawn'. One should be careful in finishing Suhoor a few minutes earlier than what is in the timetable. This is to avoid any risk of overstepping the limit.

[21] EATING SUHOOR IS DESIRABLE

عن أنس بن مالك رضي الله عنه قال: قال النبي صلى الله عليه وسلم:

تسحَّروا فإن في السحور بركة أخرجه البخاري ـ

Anas ibn Mālik ﷺ narrates that Rasūlullāh ﷺ said: "Partake from the Suhoor/pre-dawn meal, because verily there is Barakah (blessings) in Suhoor." [21]

Note: Why miss out on barkatī food? Especially when we are going to need a lot of energy throughout the day. We should make a habit of eating suhoor.

[22] SUHOOR IS A DEFINING ACT

عن عمرو بن العاص رضي الله عنه أن رسول الله صلى الله عليه وسلم قال:

---

[20] Bukhārī.
[21] Bukhārī.

فصل ما بين صيامنا وصيام أهل الكتاب أكلة السحر رواه مسلم ـ

Amr bin Āāṣ ﷺ narrates that Rasūlullāh ﷺ said, "The difference between our fasting and the fasting of Ahle Kitab, is the eating of Suhoor." [22]

Note: Ahle Kitab means 'people of the book' i.e. the Jews and the Christians. They used to fast as well, but they would not get up to eat anything for Suhoor. They would just eat something before going to sleep at night.

[23] ALLĀH AND HIS ANGELS SHOWER MERCY UPON SUHOOR TAKERS

عن عبد الله بن عمر رضي الله عنهما قال: قال رسول الله صلى الله عليه وسلم:

إن الله وملائكته يصلّون على المتسحّرين رواه ابن حبّان ـ

Abdullāh bin Umar ﷺ narrates that Rasūlullāh ﷺ said, "Indeed Allāh and His angels send mercy upon those who partake of Suhoor." [23]

Note: When we get up for suhoor, we should pray a few rak'āts of Tahajjud, do some Dhikr, read some Qur'ān and make some duās as well. All this attracts Allāh's ﷺ Rahmah.

[24] SUHOOR FOOD IS BARKATI FOOD

عن المقدام بن معد يكرب رضي الله عنه أن النبي صلى الله عليه وسلم قال:

عليكم بغداء السحور؛ فإنه هو الغداء المبارك رواه النسائي ـ

---

[22] Muslim.
[23] Ibn Ḥibbān.

Miqdam bin Made-Karab ﷺ narrates that Rasūlullāh ﷺ said, "It is imperative that you have Suhoor food, because it is indeed a blessed meal." [24]

[25] SUHOOR SHOULD BE DELAYED UP TO THE PERMITTED TIME

عن أبي الدرداء رضي الله عنه قال: قال رسول الله صلى الله عليه وسلم: ثلاث من أخلاق النبوة : تعجيل الإفطار، وتأخير السحور، ووضع اليمين على الشمال في الصلاة رواه الطبراني ـ

Abū Dardā ﷺ narrates that Rasūlullāh ﷺ said, "Three things are from the characteristics of Prophethood:

[1] To hasten in Iftaar,

[2] To delay Suhoor and,

[3] To place the right hand on the left hand in Salah." [25]

Some people do Suhoor about two hours before Subhe Sadiq. This is not Taqwā, as it goes against the Sunnah of Rasūlullāh ﷺ.

[26] TAKING A SIP OF WATER CAN BE CONSIDERED AS SUHOOR

عن عبد الله بن عمر رضي الله عنهما قال: قال رسول الله صلى الله عليه وسلم:

---

[24] Nasa'ī.
[25] Tabrānī.

33

تسحّروا ولو بجرعة من ماء رواه ابن حبّان ـ

Abdullāh bin Umar ﷺ narrates that Rasūlullāh ﷺ said: "Partake of Suhoor even though it may be a sip of water." [26]

Note: Sometimes our alarms don't go off and we get up at the last minute. We feel there is no time for suhoor, so we go back to sleep thinking we will get up later towards the end of fajr time, pray fajr and go to work. This is not right. We should at least drink a glass of water to take the Barakah of suhoor.

[27] LADIES SHOULD MAKE UP FOR THE FASTS MISSED DUE TO PERIOD

عن عائشة رضي الله عنها قالت كان يكون علي الصوم من

رمضان ، فما أستطيع أن أقضي إلا في شعبان رواه البخاري ـ

Ā'ishā ﷺ says: "Sometimes some fasts of Ramadhān would be due upon me, but I could not make up for them (qadhā) except in the month of Sha'bān. [27]

Note: This is because Rasūlullāh ﷺ would fast abundantly in the month of Sha'bān. Hadhrat Ā'ishā ﷺ says in another Hadīth that Rasūlullāh ﷺ would fast most of Sha'bān, in fact all of Sha'ban. So she would also join him and do her qadhā. We should at least fast on the 15th of Sha'bān and a few days before or after.

[28] INCREASING GENEROSITY IN RAMADHAN

عن عبد الله بن عباس رضي الله عنهما، قال: "كان رسول الله صلى الله عليه

---

[26] Ibn Ḥibbān.
[27] Bukhārī.

وسلم أجود الناس، وكان أجود ما يكون في رمضان حين يلقاه جبريل، وكان

يلقاه في كل ليلة من رمضان، فيدارسه القرآن، فلرسول الله صلى الله عليه

وسلم أجود بالخير من الريح المرسلة"، رواه البخاري ـ

Ibn Abbās ﷺ says: "Rasūlullāh ﷺ was the most generous of all people, and
he was even more generous in the month of Ramadhān when Jibra'īl ﷺ
would come to visit him. Jibra'īl ﷺ used to visit him every night of
Ramadhān and revise the Qur'ān with him. Indeed, Rasūlullāh ﷺ would be
more generous with wealth than the wind that is blowing. [28]

Note: This means that just as heavy wind blows everything away, he would
also give everything away. We normally spend more freely when we are
happy. Rasūlullāh ﷺ would be extremely happy upon the regular visits of
Jibra'īl ﷺ so he would spend everything he had or he would receive from
somewhere.

[29] SADAQAH OF RAMADHAN IS THE MOST VIRTUOUS ONE

عن أنس رضي الله عنه : سئل النبي صلى الله عليه وسلم أي الصوم أفضل بعد

رمضان؟ قال شعبان لتعظيم رمضان قال: فأي الصدقة أفضل؟ قال "صدقة في

رمضان" رواه المنذري ـ

Anas ﷺ said: Rasūlullāh ﷺ was once asked, which fast is most virtuous after
the fast of Ramadhān? He said the fast of Sha'bān in respect of Ramadhān."
He ﷺ was asked: "Which Sadaqah is the most virtuous one? He replied:
"Sadaqah during the month of Ramadhān." [29]

---

[28] Bukhārī.
[29] Munziri.

Note: Thawāb increases in Ramadhān therefore we should also increase our spending in the path of Allāh ﷻ.

[30] A SAAIM SHOULD KEEP HIS TONGUE UNDER CONTROL

عن أبي هريرة رضي الله عنه قال: إذا أصبح أحدكم يوما صائما فلا يرفث

ولا يجهل، فإن امرؤ شاتمه أو قاتله فليقل: إني صائم، إني صائم مسلم ـ

Abū Hurairah ﷺ narrates that Rasūlullāh ﷺ said, "When one of you is fasting, then he should not use obscene language, nor should he be foolish/irresponsible. And if someone swears at him or fights with him, he should say, "I am fasting." [30]

Note: Either he should say to the other person and turn away, or say it in the mind, i.e. remind himself of his duty towards the fast.

[31] ONE SHOULD NOT LIE TO ANYONE DURING THE FAST

عن أبي هريرة رضي الله عنه قال قال رسول الله صلى الله عليه وسلم من لم يدع

قول الزور والعمل به فليس لله حاجة في أن يدع طعامه وشرابه

ـ رواه البخاري ـ

---

[30] Muslim.

Abū Hurairah ﷺ narrates that Rasūlullāh ﷺ said: "Whoever does not abandon telling lies and acting upon lies, then Allāh is not in need of his abstaining from food and drink." [31]

Fasting is not just of the stomach, it is also of the other limbs. The fasting of the eyes, ears, tongue and even the heart and mind. So if a person continues with his bad habits during Sawm, it means that his Sawm is ineffective.

[32] REWARD OF SIYAAM AND QIYAM IS WIPED OUT DUE TO NOT CONTROLLING THE TONGUE

عَنْ أَبِيْ هُرَيْرَةَ عَنِ النَّبِيِّ صَلَّى اللهُ عَلَيْهِ وَسَلَّمَ ، قَالَ : " رُبَّ صَائِمٍ لَيْسَ لَهُ مِنْ صِيَامِهِ إِلا الْجُوْعُ وَرُبَّ قَائِمٍ لَيْسَ لَهُ مِنْ قِيَامِهِ إِلا السَّهَرُ رواه ابن ماجة -

Abū Hurairah ﷺ narrates that Rasūlullāh ﷺ said, "Many people fast but gain nothing from their fast except hunger and thirst. And many people stand (Qiyām-ul-Layl) but they gain nothing but sleeplessness. [32]

This is what Sayyidunā Umar ﷺ tried to explain in the following words: "The true fast is not to merely abstain from food and drink, rather a true fast is to abstain from futile activities and obscene talk." [33]

[33] BACKBITING WHILE FASTING REDUCES REWARD AND INCREASES THE EFFECTS OF HUNGER AND THIRST

---

[31] Bukhārī.
[32] Ibn Mājah.
[33] Ibn Abī Shaybah.

عَنْ عُبَيْدٍ مَوْلَى رَسُوْلِ الله صَلَّى الله عَلَيْهِ وَسَلَّم ، أَنَّ امْرَأَتَيْنِ صَامَتَا عَلَى عَهْدِ

رَسُوْلِ الله صَلَّى الله عَلَيْهِ وَسَلَّم ، فَقَالُوْا : يَا رَسُوْلَ الله ، إِنَّ هَاهُنَا امْرَأَتَيْنِ صَامَتَا

، وَقَدْ كَادَتَا أَنْ تَمُوْتَا ؟ فَقَالَ النَّبِيُّ صَلَّى الله عَلَيْهِ وَسَلَّم : "اِئْتُوْنِيْ بِهِمَا"،فَجَاءَتَا ،

فَدَعَا بِعُسٍّ أَوْ قَدَحٍ ، فَقَالَ لإِحْدَاهُمَا : " قِي " ، فَقَاءَتْ مِنْ قَيْحٍ وَدَمٍ وَصَدِيْدٍ ،

حَتَّى قَاءَتْ نِصْفَ الْقَدَحِ ، وَقَالَ لِلْأُخْرَى : " قِي " ، فَقَاءَتْ مِنْ دَمٍ وقِيْحٍ

وَصَدِيْدٍ حَتَّى مَلأَتِ الْقَدَحَ ، فَقَالَ النَّبِيُّ صَلَّى الله عَلَيْهِ وَسَلَّم : " إِنَّ هَاتَيْنِ

صَامَتَا عَمَّا أَحَلَّ اللهُ لَهُمَا ، وَأَ فْطَرَتَا عَلَى مَا حَرَّمَ اللهُ عَلَيْهِمَا ، جَلَسَتْ إِحْدَاهُمَا إِلَى

الأُخْرَى فَجَعَلَتَا تَأْكُلانِ لُحُوْمَ النَّاسِ " رواه احمد

Ubaid ﷺ, the freed slave of Rasūlullāh ﷺ, says "During the time of Rasūlullāh ﷺ, two women observed a fast for Ramadhān. A man came to Rasūlullāh ﷺ and said "Yā Rasūlullāh! There are two women who have observed fast, but they are very close to death. (Due to hunger, can they break their fast by eating something?) Rasūlullāh ﷺ said: "Go and bring them here." The two women came. Rasūlullāh ﷺ asked for a bowl, which was brought forth. He said to one of the women, "Vomit in this utensil." The woman vomited, blood and flesh came out of her mouth until she filled half the utensil. Then he said to the other woman, "Vomit in here." She did the same and she also vomited blood and flesh. Then Rasūlullāh ﷺ said,

"These two women fasted from what Allāh has made halal for them however, they broke their fast with what Allāh has made harām upon them, they sat with one another, and kept consuming the flesh of people. [34]

---

[34] Ahmed.

Note: Where did the flesh come from when their stomachs were empty? They were dying of hunger? Allāh showed people a miracle that backbiting, in reality, is like eating the flesh of the other person.

[34] A SAAIM IS ALLOWED TO KISS HIS WIFE, PROVIDED HE CONTROLS HIMSELF

عن عائشة رضي الله عنها قالت: كان رسول الله صلى الله عليه وسلم يقبِّل وهو صائم، ويباشر وهو صائم، ولكنه أملَكُكُم لأَرَبه. أخرجه البخاري ـ

Ā'ishā ﷺ says: "Rasūlullāh ﷺ used to kiss, hug and embrace (his wives) while fasting, and he had more control of his desires than any of you." [35]

[35] EATING BY MISTAKE, WHILE FORGETTING THE FAST, DOES NOT BREAK IT

عن أبي هريرة رضي الله عنه قال: قال رسول الله صلى الله عليه وسلم: من نسي وهو صائم فأكل أو شرب فليتمَّ صومه؛ فإنما أطعمه الله وسقاه أخرجه البخاري ـ

Abū Hurairah ﷺ narrates that Rasūlullāh ﷺ said: "When a fasting person forgets and eats and drinks, then he should complete his fast, because Allāh has fed him and Allāh has given him drink." [36]

---

[35] Bukhārī.
[36] Bukhārī.

[36] VOMIT ITSELF DOES NOT BREAK FAST, UNLESS IT'S ATTEMPTED AND DELIBERATE

عن أبي هريرة رضي الله عنه أن النبي صلى الله عليه وسلم قال:
من ذَرَعه القيء فليس عليه قضاء، ومن استقاء عمدًا فليقضِ أخرجه أحمد
وأبو داود ـ

Abū Hurairah ﷺ narrates that Rasūlullāh ﷺ said, "Whoever is over-powered by vomit, there is no qadhā upon him (i.e. the fast is still valid). However, if one induces vomit, then upon him is qadhā." [37]

[37] BEING CAREFUL IN SAWM WHEN GARGLING AND CLEANING THE NOSE

عن لقيط بن صبرة رضي الله عنه قال: قلت: يا رسول الله، أخبرني عن
الوضوء، قال: أسغ الوضوء، وخلِّل بين الأصابع، وبالغ في الاستنشاق إلا أن
تكون صائمًا رواه أحمد ـ

Laqīt Ibn Sabira ﷺ says I asked Rasūlullāh ﷺ to tell me about Wudhū! He said: Do Wudhū thoroughly and do khilāl in between the fingers and strive hard in putting water up the nose (and flushing it), except when you are fasting. [38]

Note: Because of the risk of water going up the nose and down in the throat, which would then break the fast.

---

[37] Ahmed, Abū Dāwūd.
[38] Ahmed.

[38] FASTING DURING TRAVELLING IS PERMITTED

عن حمزة بن عمرو الأسلمي رضي الله عنه أنه قال: يا رسول الله، أجد بي قوة

على الصيام في السفر، فهل عليَّ جناح؟ فقال رسول الله صلى الله عليه وسلم:

هي رخصة من الله، فمن أخذ بها فحسن، ومن أحبَّ أن يصوم فلا جناح عليه

أخرجه البخاري ـ

Hamzā Al-Aslamī ﷺ narrates that he said: Yā Rasūlullāh! I have the energy to fast while travelling, Is there anything wrong in this? Rasūlullāh ﷺ said: It (to not fast during travelling) is a Rukhsat (dispensation) from Allāh. Whoever takes it, it is good and whosoever would like to fast, there is no harm. [39]

Note: Some people say it is harām to fast while travelling. Even if such people go for Umrah to Makkāh Mukarramah, during Ramadhān, they don't fast. This Hadīth proves them wrong. They should fast, especially in this day and age where travelling is much easier in comparison to the previous eras.

[39] WHILE TRAVELLING, A SAAIM TRAVELLER SHOULD NOT LOOK DOWN ON A NON−SAAIM TRAVELLER

عن أبي سعيد الخدري وجابر بن عبد الله رضي الله عنهم قالا: سافرنا مع

رسول الله صلى الله عليه وسلم فيصوم الصائم، ويفطر المفطر، فلا يعيب

بعضهم على بعض. أخرجه مسلم ـ

---

[39] Bukhārī.

Abū Saeed ﷺ and Jābir ﷺ relate that we were traveling with Rasūlullāh ﷺ. While we were on the journey, some observed the fast, and others didn't. They did not blame each other, i.e. the ones who fasted didn't look down on those who didn't. And those who didn't, didn't blame those who did fast." [40]

[40] BREAKING A FAST OF RAMADHĀN FOR NO REASON, CANNOT BE ATONED FOR

عَنْ أَبِيْ هُرَيْرَةَ قَالَ : قَالَ رَسُوْلُ الله صَلَّى الله عَلَيْهِ وَسَلَّمَ مَنْ أَفْطَرَ يَوْمًا مِنْ رَمَضَانَ مِنْ غَيْرِ عُذْرٍ وَلَا مَرَضٍ لَمْ يَقْضِهِ صِيَامُ الدَّهْرِ وِاِنْ صَامَهُ . رواه المنذري والبخاري في العلل وقال إبن بطال : ضعيف ـ

"Whoever breaks/fails to observe one day of the fast of Ramadhān, without a valid excuse, or any illness, fasting throughout their whole life wouldn't be enough to compensate for it, even if he were to do so. [41]

Note: This means he won't be able to recover the Thawāb of that single fast in any way. He does have to make qadhā if he missed it or even pay Kaffārah if he deliberately broke it.

[41] WHERE POSSIBLE, FAST SHOULD BE OPENED WITH A DATE

عن سليمان بن عامر عن النبي صلى الله عليه وسلم أنه قال: إذا أفطر أحدكم، فليفطر على تمر فإنه بركة، فإن لم يجد تمرًا، فالماء فإنه طهور رواه الترمذي،

---

[40] Muslim.
[41] Bukhārī.

Sulaimān bin Āamir ⬡ narrates that Rasūlullāh ⬡ said: "When one of you intends to break his fast, he should open it with a date because a date is full of blessings, if he cannot find a date, he should open his fast with water, because water is cleansing (purifying)." [42]

This means opening at sunset, when the fast has completed.

[42] DUĀ FOR IFTAAR

دعاء الإفطار :

عن معاذ بن زهرة قال : إن النبي صلى الله عليه وسلم كان إذا أفطر قال :

" اللهم لك صمت وعلى رزقك أفطرت " رواه أبو داود مرسلا ـ

Muāz Ibn Zahra ⬡ reports that when Rasūlullāh ⬡ broke his fast, he would say: "O Allāh! For you did I fast and with your given sustenance do I break it." [43]

كَانَ رَسُوْلُ اللهِ صَلَّى اللهُ عَلَيْهِ وَسَلَّمَ إِذَا أَفْطَرَ قَالَ ذَهَبَ الظَّمَأُ

وَابْتَلَّتِ الْعُرُوْقُ وَثَبَتَ الْأَجْرُ إِنْ شَاءَ اللهُ رواه ابو داود ـ

Another narration mentions that he would say: "The thirst is quenched, the veins are replenished, and hopefully the reward is set, by the will of Allāh." [44]

---

[42] Tirmīdhī.
[43] Abū Dāwūd, Mursal.
[44] Abū Dāwūd.

[43] STAYING AWAKE AT NIGHT
DURING THE LAST ASHARAH

عن عائشة رضي الله عنها قالت: كان النبي صلى الله عليه وسلم إذا دخل

العشر شدَّ مئزره وأحيا ليله، وأيقظ أهله. أخرجه البخاري ومسلم ـ

Āʾisha 🐝 reports: "When the last ten days of Ramadhān would begin,
Rasūlullāh 🐝 would tighten his garment, and stay awake at night and
awaken his family." [45]

Tightening the garment could mean staying away from his wives to keep
busy in Ibādah. It could be a phrase used to say he would get ready to work
hard.

[44] PERFORMING I'TIKĀF
IN THE LAST ASHARAH

عَنْ عَائِشَةَ رضي الله عنها كان رسول الله صلى الله عليه وسلم

يعتكف العشر الأواخر من رمضان اخرجه البخاري ـ

Āʾisha 🐝 reports: Rasūlullāh 🐝 would perform I'tikāf in the
last ten days of Ramadhān. [46]

---

[45] Bukhārī, Muslim.
[46] Bukhārī.

[45] EXTRA EFFORT IN THE
LAST 10 DAYS OF RAMADHĀN

عن عائشة رضي الله عنها قالت: كان رسول الله صلى الله عليه وسلم

يجتهد في العشر الأواخر ما لا يجتهد في غيره أخرجه مسلم ـ

Ā'ishā 🌸 reports: Rasūlullāh 🌸 would strive [to do acts of worship] during the last ten days of Ramadhān more than he would in any other time. [47]

[46] SEARCHING FOR LAYLATUL QADR

عن عائشة رضي الله عنها أن رسول الله صلى الله عليه وسلم قال:

تحروا ليلة القدر في الوتر من العشر الأواخر من رمضان أخرجه البخاري ـ

Ā'ishā 🌸 narrates that Rasūlullāh 🌸 said: "Search for Laylatul Qadr in the odd nights from the last 10 nights of Ramadhān." [48]

[47] GRAVE WARNING FOR NEGLECTING
THE MONTH OF RAMADHĀN

حَدَّثَنِي سَعْدُ بْنُ إِسْحَاقَ بْنِ كَعْبِ بْنِ عُجْرَةَ، عَنْ أَبِيهِ، عَنْ كَعْبِ بْنِ عُجْرَةَ،

قَالَ: قَالَ رَسُولُ الله صَلَّى اللهُ عَلَيْهِ وَسَلَّمَ: " احْضُرُوا المِنْبَرَ " فَحَضَرْنَا، فَلَمَّا

ارْتَقَى دَرَجَةً قَالَ: " آمِينَ "، فَلَمَّا ارْتَقَى الدَّرَجَةَ الثَّانِيَةَ قَالَ: " آمِينَ "، فَلَمَّا

---

[47] Muslim.
[48] Bukhārī.

ارْتَقَى الدَّرَجَةَ الثَّالِثَةَ قَالَ: " آمِينَ "، فَلَمَّا فَرَغَ نَزَلَ مِنَ المِنْبَرِ قَالَ: فَقُلْنَا له يَا

رَسُولَ الله لَقَدْ سَمِعْنَا الْيَوْمَ مِنْكَ شَيْئًا لَمْ نَكُنْ نَسْمَعُهُ قَالَ: " إِنَّ جِبْرِيلَ عَلَيْهِ

السَّلَامِ عَرَضَ لِي فَقَالَ: بَعُدَ مَنْ أَدْرَكَ رَمَضَانَ فَلَمْ يُغْفَرْ لَهُ فَقُلْتُ: آمِينَ فَلَمَّا

رَقِيتُ الثَّانِيَةَ قَالَ: بَعُدَ مَنْ ذُكِرْتَ عِنْدَهُ فَلَمْ يُصَلِّ عَلَيْكَ فَقُلْتُ: آمِينَ، فَلَمَّا

رَقِيتُ الثَّالِثَةَ قَالَ: بَعُدَ مَنْ أَدْرَكَ وَالِدَيْهِ الْكِبَرَ عِنْدَهُ أَوْ أَحَدُهُمَا، فَلَمْ يُدْخِلَاهُ

الجَنَّةَ – أَظُنُّهُ قَالَ – فَقُلْتُ: آمِينَ "

Ka'b Ibn Ujrah ﷺ says: Once Rasūlullāh ﷺ said: "Come close to the mimbar." We did accordingly. He ﷺ ascended the pulpit and said "Āmīn" on the first step, then again " Āmīn" on the second step and then " Āmīn" on the third step. When he descended, we asked him, "We heard something from you which we don't normally hear." He ﷺ said: Jibra'īl ﷺ appeared before me, and said, "May that person be distanced who despite obtaining the month of Ramadhān, was still not forgiven." I said, "Āmīn." When I ascended the second step he said, "May that person be distanced in whose presence you are mentioned but he does not confer blessings upon you." I said, " Āmīn." When I ascended the third step, he said, "Woe unto that person whose parents reach old age in his presence, yet he does not obtain Jannah (by serving them). I said, " Āmīn." [49]

Note: This means that those three are great blessings of Allāh ﷻ. Ramadhān, Rasūlullāh ﷺ and elderly parents. When someone violates their rights, they invite the curse of Allāh ﷻ. May Allāh ﷻ protect us. Āmīn.

---

[49] Baihaqī.

[48] KEEPING 6 NAFL FASTS OF SHAWWĀL

عن أبي أيوب الأنصاري رضي الله عنه أن رسول الله صلى الله عليه وسلم قال:

من صام رمضان ثم أتبعه ستًا من شوال، كان كصيام الدهر رواه مسلم -

Abū Ayyūb Al-Anṣārī ﷺ narrates that Rasūlullāh ﷺ said: "Whosoever fasts
in Ramadhān, then follows it up by six fast of Shawwāl, it is as though he
has kept fasts throughout the whole year. [50]

Note: This is because the reward of one deed is multiplied ten times, so 36
will be like 360. It is desirable (Mustahabb) to keep the six fasts of Shawwāl.
Ladies cannot combine the six of Shawwāl with their Qadhā of Ramadhān.
They both have to be kept separately. It's like 4 Sunnah's of Zuhr and 4 Fardh.
One cannot combine them both.

MASĀ'IL OF FASTING

These are a few Masā'il regarding fasting. May Allāh ﷺ make them beneficial!
Āmīn. I have gone over them with three doctors: Doctor Mazharuddin Sahib,
Doctor Salīm and Doctor Liaqat. I also had them checked by our respected
Muftī Shabbīr Sahib (Dāmat Barakātuhum).

DEFINITION

Sawm literally means 'to restrain oneself'. In Sharī'ah terminology, it means
to refrain from these things throughout the day, eating, drinking and
deriving sexual pleasure. Fasting is a great form of worship. One Hadīth says:
"Everything has a door and the door of worship is fasting." It elevates a
person from the animalistic nature to angelic ones.

---

[50] Muslim.

WHERE THE SUN DOES NOT SET OR RISE

There are countries in the world where the sun does not set for six months and it doesn't rise for the other six months. The Fuqahā say that the people of these countries should fast according to the timings of countries close to them. [51]

LONG HOURS

During the summer months, we have very long fasts. We should think of the short winter fasts we used to keep. When Allāh ﷻ made it easy for us during winter, then if Allāh ﷻ tests us a little bit in summer, we should accept Allāh's ﷻ order wholeheartedly. Some people find loopholes to avoid fasting. That should not be the case.

Some people claim to be diabetic and eat and drink freely in front of others who are fasting. If the person is elderly and a heavy diabetic, it could be understood. But many are healthy, go to work, or roam around the streets all day, smoke in the streets during Ramadhān etc. Such people should check their Imān.

UPON WHOM IS FASTING COMPULSORY ?

There are only three conditions for fasting to be Fardh:

[1] Islam
[2] Sanity
[3] Bulūgh (i.e. being mature)

When a person is Muslim, sane and mature, he/she has to fast. The only other condition is that he/she should not be a mā'zūr (a person who has a genuine excuse such as severe illness where there is no possibility of recovering).

---

[51] قلت: وكذلك يقدر لجميع الآجال كالصوم والزكاة (شامي)

WHEN DOES FASTING HAVE TO BE POSTPONED FOR A LATER DATE ?

[1] Haidh
[2] Nifaas

A woman on her period or post-natal bleeding is not permitted to fast. She has to postpone fasting for other days.

GENUINE EXCUSES FOR NOT FASTING OR POSTPONING

[1] Being sick
[2] A traveller
[3] Pregnant
[4] Breastfeeding
[5] Extreme weakness which can lead to illness
[6] Insanity
[7] Being unconscious for long periods, as in coma
[8] Being in the battlefield, striving for the cause of Allāh ﷻ

When these excuses finish, one has to fast. If illness continues and the person is unable to make Qadhā at a later date, then they have to give fidyā, which is the amount of Sadaqatul Fitr for every missed fast.

NIYYAH

Intention is in the heart. It does not have to be said verbally. Eating Suhoor is an indication of the intent. However, if one does want to make a verbal intention, there is no reason to stop them. One could say:

وبصوم غد نويت من شهر رمضان ـ

"I intend to fast tomorrow for Ramadhān."

If one stays hungry and thirsty, without intending to fast, the fast will not be counted.

Note:

[1] One should try to keep all fasts properly. If one breaks a fast or does not keep it at all, it is impossible to gain the reward, which could equal that of the missed fast. One Hadīth says:

من أفطر يوما من رمضان من غير رخصة ولا

مرض لم يقض عنه صوم الدهر كله وان صامه ٥٢

"Whoever misses (or breaks) a fast of Ramadhān without a genuine reason, or any sickness, fasting for the whole life cannot make up for it, even if he were to do so." [53]

[2] One needs to keep a golden rule in mind:

الفطر مما دخل وليس مما خرج ٥٤

"A fast breaks by what goes in the body, not by what comes out."

Therefore, if one has a blood test, or a diabetic person checks his sugar level, or someone has cupping done (Hijāmah) etc, his fast will not be broken. It will be broken by something which enters the cavity of the body, i.e. which goes either down the throat into the stomach or into the brain. This can be through the throat, nose, ears, anus or the private parts.

However, there are two exceptions:

---

[52] رواه المنذرى عن ابى هريرة مرفوعا

[53] Munziri.

[54] رواه البخارى عن ابن عباس ورواه البيهقى مرفوعا ورواه ابو يعلى الموصلى عن عائشة مرفوعا

[1] القىٔ vomiting: If one intentionally and deliberately draws vomit from the stomach (by sticking a finger down his throat, applying pressure to his stomach or deliberately smelling a repulsive odour) and it is a mouthful, the fast will be broken – there is a consensus upon this. If the vomit was less than a mouthful, then Imām Muhammad's ﷺ research is that it will still be broken. However, Imām Abū Yūsuf ﷺ says it will NOT be broken. Ihtiyaat (caution) will be to take Imām Muhammad's ﷺ opinion. Allāmah Aynī ﷺ writes:

" الأصل فى العبادات الاحتياط " [55]

وان إستقاء أى طلب القىٔ عامدا اى متذكرا لصومه ان كان ملأ الفم فسد

بالإجماع مطلقا. وإن أقلّ لا عند الثانى وهو الصحيح لكن ظاهر الرواية كقول

محمد انه يفسد كما فى الفتح عن الكافى. [56]

وعن ابى هريرة رضى الله عنه قال قال رسول الله من ذرعه القىٔ

وهو صائم فليس عليه قضاء وان استقاء عمدا فليقض [57]

If the vomiting was UNINTENTIONAL and without the person's own doing, it does NOT break the fast, even if it was a mouthful.

If part of the vomit goes back down the throat, then if it went back down on its own, the fast is not broken. However, if it was deliberately swallowed, the fast is broken.

اذا قاء او استقاء ملء الفم او دونه وعاد بنفسه او اعاد

او اخرج فلا فطر على الاصح الا فى الاعادة [58]

---

[55] البناية ص 1400/ 2

[56] شامى ص 393/ 3 تحفة ص 68

[57] رواه الترمذى وابو داود. احكا رمضان ص 287

[58] هندية ص 204/ 1 تحفة ص 66

[2] المنى Semen: If semen comes out of the body due to sexual intercourse or masturbation, or any other deliberate activity, the fast will be broken, similarly, if there was no intercourse, just foreplay of hugging and kissing, which resulted in semen coming out, the fast will break.

$$...أَوْ قَبَّلَ وَلَوْ قُبْلَةً فَاحِشَةً بِأَنْ يُدَغْدِغُ أَوْ يَمُصُّ شَفَتَيْهَا (أَوْ لَمَسَ) وَلَوْ بِحَائِلٍ لَا يَمْنَعُ الْحَرَارَةَ...(فَأَنْزَلَ).. قَضَى فِي الصُّوَرِ كُلِّهَا ^{59}$$

However, if one forgot he was fasting and had sexual intercourse, or had a wet dream and semen came out, or semen was released just by looking, or thinking and without any physical action, the fast will NOT break.

$$منها لو أكل الصائم او شرب او جامع ناسيا لصومه ^{60}$$
$$او احتلم..الخ لم يفطر ^{61}$$

Note: المنى or semen is that thick sticky substance which is released upon ejaculation, followed by loosening of the organ. There is another substance called المذى Mazī. This is some discharge which is released during foreplay or upon thinking of the act. There is no ejaculation involved. This sticky discharge does not break the fast.

$$إِذا مص الصائم امرأته وأمذى لا يفسد صومه ^{62}$$

شامى ص 379 / 3 فتاوى دار العلوم ص 417 / 6 تحفة ص 70 ^{59}

مراقى الفلاح ص 360 تحفة ص 62 ^{60}

شامى ص 367 / 3 تحفة ص 63 ^{61}

تاتارخانية ص 371 / 2 أحسن الفتاوى ص 441 / 4 ^{62}

وكذا إذا نظر إلى امرأة فأمنى لما بينا فصار كالمتفكر اذا أمنى [6463]

Note: لواطة . If two homosexuals perform the act of intercourse, their fast will be broken. Both will have to keep Qadhā and give Kaffārah.

ثم عندنا كما تجب الكفارة بالوقاع على الرجل تجب على المرأة ـ

قوله "تجب على المرأة" قال على المفعول به كان افيه . [65]

Note: Homosexual acts are harām and a major sin in the eyes of Allāh ﷻ.

We now put forward an anatomy of the body to explain what breaks the fast and what doesn't.

MOUTH

If someone went to the dentist for cleaning, for a filling, or for extracting a tooth, his or her fast is at a huge risk. There is the possibility that some liquid or blood could go down the throat. It is nearly impossible to avoid it so the fast will be broken. If bleeding from the gums occurs both spontaneously or as a result of treatment, and the blood went down the throat, the fast will be broken (though it wouldn't break if one spat it out) and nothing went down the throat.

Swallowing capsules or pain killer tablets will break the fast. However, if the medicine was in liquid form and just a drop was placed on the tongue, it dissolved on the tongue and did not go down the throat, it will not break the fast.[66] This can be the case with some homeopathic medicines, or an angina tablet which is placed under the tongue. [67]

---

[63] الهداية مع فتح القدير ص 333 / 2

[64] احكام ص 391

[65] الهداية و فتح القدير ص 342 / 2

[66] أحكام ص 227

[67] الفتاوى اللُّجنَة

Swallowing saliva mixed with blood, where the blood is more than the saliva, will break the fast. Likewise, swallowing another person's saliva (such as the wife's after kissing), or one's own saliva after taking it out in the hand and then licking it, will break the fast (not if it was still in the mouth). If something edible was stuck between the teeth, one should spit it out. However, if one swallowed it without taking it out of the mouth, and it was smaller than a chickpea, the fast will not break. If it was larger, or smaller but one took it out in the hand and then put it back in the mouth to swallow it, the fast will break.

وَإِنْ أَكَلَ مَا بَيْنَ أَسْنَانِهِ لَمْ يُفْسِدْ إِنْ كَانَ قَلِيلًا وَإِنْ كَانَ كَثِيرًا يُفْسِدُ، وَالْحِمَّصَةُ وَمَا فَوْقَهَا كَثِيرٌ، وَمَا دُونَهَا قَلِيلٌ، وَإِنْ أَخْرَجَهُ وَأَخَذَهُ بِيَدِهِ ثُمَّ أَكَلَ يَنْبَغِيَ أَنْ يُفْسِدَ[68]

If there was some wetness left in the mouth after gargling and throwing the water out, and it went down the throat with the saliva, it will not break the fast.

ولو بقى بلل بعد مضمضة فابتلعه مع البزاق لم يفطر[69]

Swallowing a stone, mud, metal or anything that is not edible will break the fast. However, if a fly or a mosquito went down the throat whilst yawning, the fast will not break. Similarly, if particles of Miswaak remained in the mouth and went down despite the effort to spit it out, the fast will not break.

The fast will break by water going down the throat whilst gargling, even by mistake. This is important to remember whilst doing Wudhū or Ghusl. Gargle lightly. One Hadīth says:

---

[68] الفتاوى الهندية ص 252 / 1 تحفة ص 64

[69] هندية ص 203 / 1 تحفة ص 65

وبالغ فى المضمضة الا ان تكون صائما ⁷⁰

However, according to Imām Shāfi'ee's ﷺ research, the fast will not break by such mistakes.

If someone was forced to eat or drink, by an enemy or due to fear of life, or he fell ill whilst fasting and the doctors administered some medicine, the fast will be broken, though only Qadhā will be necessary, not Kaffārah. Chewing gum, Paan (betel leaves), tobacco, Niswaar etc. will also break the fast. [71]

If someone was chewing Paan, fell asleep with the Paan in his mouth, and woke up after Subhe Sadiq, his fast will not be counted. If someone gargled after having Paan but some reddish colour was left and went down the throat with the saliva, it will not break the fast.

وان أفطر خطأ كان تمضمض فسبقه الماء او شرب نائما قضى فقط ⁷²

Blood from a nose bleed which goes down the throat will break the fast.

اذا دخل رُفَاعُهُ حلقه فسد صومه ⁷³

SMOKING CIGARETTES

Smoking cigarettes or cigars breaks the fast. With regards to Kaffārah along with Qadhā, there are two opinions of the Muftiyāne Kirām.

[1] Muftī Salmān Mansūrpūrī is of the opinion that only Qadhā is necessary, not Kaffārah. He writes:

---

⁷⁰ ذكره ابن العربى فى عارضة الاحوذى ص 189 / 2

⁷¹ احكام ص 258

⁷² شامى زكريا ص 373 / 2 تحفة ص 68

⁷³ تاتارخانية ص 369 / 2 تحفة ص 68

وبه علم حكم شرب الدخان ونظمه الشرنبلالى فى شرحه

على الوهبانية بقوله "وشاربه فى الصوم لا شكّ يفطر" [74]

[2] However, Muftī Radhāul Haq Sahib of Dārul Uloom Zakarīyā writes that Kaffārah will also be Wājib. This is the opinion of our Muftī Shabbīr Sahib and Muftī Sūfī Tāhir Sahib.

مفتی رضاء الحق کہتے ہیں عام طور سے سیگریٹ پینے والے سیگریٹ کو نفع بخش سمجھتے ہیں لہذا قضاء و کفارہ دونوں لازم ہیں۔ اور پاس بیٹھنے والا حلق میں دھواں کھینچ کر داخل کرے [75] تو (اسکا بھی) روزہ فاسد ہو جائیگا اور قضاء واجب ہو گی۔

Muftī Radhāul Haq says, "Usually those who smoke cigarettes do so because they know it benefits them, thus Qadhā and Kaffārah will both become necessary. Also, if someone who was sitting next to a smoker intentionally draws in the smoke, his fast will also break and Qadhā will be necessary."

قال الشرنبلالى ويلزمه التكفير لو ظن نافعا وكذا قال الطحطاوى حاشيته على المراقى ص 665

وعلى هذا البدعة التى ظهرت الآن وهو الدخان إذا شربه فى لزوم الكفارة فمن قال اذا التغذى ما يميل اليه الطبع وتنقض به شهوة البطن ألزم به الكفارة. انتهى...

---

[74] شامى زكريا ص 366 / 3 فتاوى دار العاوم ص 365 / 6 تحفة ص 69

[75] Passive Smoking.

SMOKING HUQQA OR SHISHA

Smoking Huqqa or Shisha, will also break the fast, Qadhā will be necessary and in some cases Kaffārah also becomes necessary. This is when something beneficial is added to it e.g. fruit flavourings etc.

حقہ سے روزہ ٹوٹ جاتا ہے اور قضاء لازم ہوتی ہے بعض صورتوں میں کفارہ بھی لازم ہوتا ہے یعنی اسے نفع بخش سمجھا تو کفارہ قضاء دونوں لازم ہونگے ورنہ صرف قضاء [76]

If smoke goes down the throat without any wrongdoing, the fast will not break e.g. while cooking in the kitchen.

او دخل حلقہ غبار او ذباب او دخان ولو ذاکرا استحسانا [77]

ASTHMA PUMP

If someone had an asthma attack and used the asthma pump, the fast will be broken according to the Hanafī research. This is because the pump contains medicine, which goes down the throat. [78] [79]

Some people say that it does not break the fast, because the medicine goes into the lungs, not down to the stomach. However, this is not true. The Fuqahā have said that smoking cigarettes breaks the fast, and that smoke also goes down to the lungs and not the stomach. Therefore, anything that is swallowed or inhaled deliberately should nullify the fast. Secondly, although most of it goes in the lungs, some of it does go down the throat and into the stomach.

---

[76] فتاوی دارالعلوم دیوبند ص 6/419

[77] شامی زکریا 366 / 3 بیروت 367 / 3 تحفۃ ص 63

[78] قاری عبد الباسط

[79] محمد. احکام رمضان المبارک ص 228

One may ask, "What should such a person do?" The answer would be to try and avoid the pump as much as possible. Avoid heavy activities, which make one short of breath – take it easy during Ramadhān. If one can take time off during Ramadhān they should do so. Then, if it becomes necessary to take it, use it, but do Tashabbuh Bissaimeen i.e. emulate those who are fasting and keep Qadhā during the shorter days of winter.

If the person is elderly or unable to keep Qadhā, he/she could give Fidyā for the fasts.

LOCAL ANAESTHETIC

Local anaesthetic either applied to the skin or injected into the body will not break the fast. General anaesthetic gases given through the mouth and nose would break the fast if there is some other solution mixed in them, which normally is the case. [80]

USE OF OXYGEN

If someone needs oxygen and has to take it while moving around, this will not break the fast, because it is just air compressed in a bottle and taken to ease the breathing. There is no substance in it. [81]

USING PERFUME

If someone sprayed perfume on himself, he felt the taste of it in his throat, this will not break the fast. [82]

TASTING FOOD

To taste food or to chew it and then throw it out without anything going down the throat is Makrūh if there is no genuine reason (Udhr). If it was done due to a genuine reason, it will not be Makrūh. In both cases the fast will not break. A genuine reason could be an ill-tempered husband who could get

---

[80] فتاوى اللُّجْنَة

[81] جديد فقهي مسائل ص 128 أحكام ص 227

[82] أحكام 227

very angry at the wife if the salt or masala was not proper. Chefs working in restaurants could also be excused if the boss is a hot-tempered person and the job could be at risk if mistakes are made. However, it would be better to have it tasted by a non-Muslim colleague. One should avoid putting the fast at risk. [83]

TEARS OR SWEAT

Tears or sweat going down the throat. If just a drop or two went down and no salty taste is felt in the throat, the fast will not break. However, if it was a lot, or a little but the taste was felt, it will break.

اذا دخل الدمع فى فم الصائم ان كان قليلا نحو القطرة او القطرتين لا يفسد

صومه لان الإحتراز عنه غير ممكن. وان كان كثيرا حتى وجد ملوحته فى جميع

فمه وابتلعه فسد صومه وكذا الجواب فى عرق الوجه [84]

GINGIVITIS

This is where the gums constantly bleed and sometimes blood goes down the throat, will this break the fast? If one spits the blood out, it will not affect the fast. However, if one swallows it and the blood was more than the saliva or equal to it, the fast will break. If blood was only minimal, the fast will not break, unless he felt the taste of the blood when he swallowed it.

لو خرج الدم من بين اسنانه ودخل حلقه يفسد لم يصل الى جوفه.

أما اذا وصل فان غلب الدم او تساويا فسد والا لا إلا اذا وجد طعمه [85]

[83] أحكام ص 229

[84] أحكام 3 / ص 178 ص المى

[85] شامى ص 367 / 3 احكام ص 234

EXTRACTING THE TOOTH WHILST FASTING

If one's tooth was loose and it came out or it was extracted smoothly without any bleeding, the fast will not break. However, if it involved bleeding and blood went down the throat, it will break the fast. Qadhā will be necessary.

قلت ومن هذا يُعلم من قلع ضرسه فى رمضان ودخل الدم الى جوفه فى النهار

ولو نائمًا فيجب عليه القضاء [86]

BRUSHING THE TEETH WITH TOOTHPASTE

It is Makrūh to brush the teeth with toothpaste, or use mouthwash whilst fasting. This is because of the taste of the paste and because of the risk of something going down the throat. If something did go down the throat, it will break the fast as well. One should use a Miswaak. If the Miswaak was fresh and it had a pleasant taste that would not harm the fast. It will not even be Makrūh, nor will it affect the fast.

وكره له ذوق شىء ومضغه [87]

ولا بأس بالسواك الرطب واليابس فى الغداة والعشى ولا يكره الكحل

ولا دهن شاربه كذا فى الكنز [88]

WOMEN APPLYING LIPSTICK

If there is risk that the lipstick will go down the throat at some stage, it will be Makrūh to apply. If it does go down the throat, it will break the fast, otherwise it won't. [89]

---

[86] شامى ص 368 / 3 أحكام ص 233

[87] شامى بيروت ص 352 / 3 فتاوى دار العلوم ص 404 / 6 تحفة ص 74

[88] علمجيرى ص 199 / 1 جواهر الفقه ص 379 / 1 تحفة ص 26

[89] تحفة ص 74

NOSE

If one was cleaning the nose in Wudhū or Ghusl, and he pulled the water up his nose so hard that it went down the throat, his fast will be broken.

If one snuffed some medicine up his nose or sniffed some drugs or glue etc. his fast will be broken. Similarly, if one used Bukhoor and deliberately took smoke up his nose, his fast will be broken.

لو ادخل حلقه الدخان اى بأى صورة كان أفطر لامكان التحرز عنه ٩٠

If one had the flu and put some Vicks in a bucket of hot water and inhaled the steam into his nose by covering his head with a towel or something, his fast will be broken.

EARS

If one was to put some medicine, eardrops or oil inside his ears, the fast will break. This could be because the substance travels up to the brain and nullifies the fast. Only Qadhā will be necessary, not Kaffārah.

ومن احتقن او استعط او أقطر فى أذنه أفطر ولا كفارة عليه ٩١

If someone cleaned the ears with cotton buds or pierced something in the ears and took some dirt out, the fast will not be broken. Even if one re-entered the piece with the dirt stuck to it, the fast will not break.

واذا حكّ اذنه بعود فأخرج العود وعلى رأسه شئ من الدّرن ثم أدخل

ثانيا مع ذلك الدرن ثم أخرجه وبقى الدرن فى الأذن لا يفسد ٩٢

شامى ص 366 / 3 تحفة ص 67 ٩٠

هداية ص 220 / 1 ٩١

الفتاوى تاتارخانية ص 364 / 2 شامى ص 367 / 3 أحكام ص 251 ٩٢

If water went into the ears, it will be one of two scenarios:

[1] It went inside without any wrongdoing from the person. E.g. one jumped into a swimming pool or river, or one was having a shower and water went into the ear by mistake. This will not break the fast as there is no intent here and water is not something, which does good to the ears. Plus, it is normally unavoidable, so Sharī'ah will be flexible.

[2] However, if one deliberately thrusts water inside, or puts medicine or oil, then the Saheeh Qowl (correct opinion) is that the fast will break.

صائم اغتسل فدخل الماء فى أذنه لا شىء عليه لانه لم يوجد الفطر صورة ولا معنى [93]

قال الشامى إن دخل لا يفسد وان أدخله يفسد فى الصحيح لانه وصل الى الجوف بفعله فلا يعتبر فيه صلاح البدن [94]

قال قاضيخان ولو خاض الماء فدخل الماء أذنه لا يفسد صومه. وان صب الماء فى أذنه اختلفوا فيه والصحيح الفساد لانه وصل الى الجوف بفعله فلا يعتبر فيه صلاح البدن [95]

EYES

If someone applied eye drops or artificial tears to the eyes, this will not invalidate the fast, as there is no direct passage from the eyes to the stomach or the brain.

---

[93] الفتاوى الغياثية ص 53 أحكام ص 252

[94] شامى ص 367 / 3

[95] الفتاوى الخانية مع الهندية ص 209 / 1 احكام ص 254

قال الكاسانى انه ليس للعين منفذ الى الجوف [96]

If one applied Surmah (Kohl) to the eyes, the fast will not break, even if he felt the taste in his throat or the colour appeared in the saliva. This is because it is narrated in the Hadīth that Rasūlullāh ﷺ applied Surmah whilst he was fasting.

عَنْ عَائِشَةَ، قَالَتْ : اكْتَحَلَ رَسُولُ اللهِ صَلَّى اللهُ عَلَيْهِ وَسَلَّمَ وَهُوَ صَائِمٌ [97]

عَنْ أَنَسِ بْنِ مَالِكٍ قَالَ : جَاءَ رَجُلٌ إِلَى النَّبِيِّ صَلَّى اللهُ عَلَيْهِ وَسَلَّمَ فَقَالَ: اشْتَكَتْ عَيْنِي، أَفَأَكْتَحِلُ وَأَنَا صَائِمٌ ؟ قَالَ: نَعَمْ. [98]

قَالَ الكَاسَانِى وَلَا بَأْسَ أَنْ يَكْتَحِلَ الصَّائِمُ بِالإِثْمِدِ وَغَيْرِهِ، وَلَوْ فَعَلَ لَا يُفْطِرُهُ وَإِنْ وَجَدَ طَعْمَهُ فِي حَلْقِهِ عِنْدَ عَامَّةِ الْعُلَمَاءِ لِمَا رَوَيْنَا «أَنَّ رَسُولَ اللهِ – صَلَّى اللهُ عَلَيْهِ وَسَلَّمَ – اكْتَحَلَ وَهُوَ صَائِمٌ» وَلِمَا ذَكَرْنَا أَنَّهُ لَيْسَ لِلْعَيْنِ مَنْفَذٌ إِلَى الْجَوْفِ [99]

PRIVATE PARTS

Sexual intercourse breaks the fast. Whether ejaculation takes place or not, is irrelevant. Both parties will have to keep Qadhā and give Kaffārah as well.

If someone masturbates whilst fasting, the fast will break. Qadhā will be Wājib, not Kaffārah. Kaffārah not being Fardh is because deriving sexual pleasure is only complete when two parties are involved, so the effect is also lessened when no one else is involved.

---

[96] بدائع الصنائع ص 635 / 2

[97] ابن ماجه 1678

[98] ترمذى 726 . احكام ص 219

[99] بدائع ص 635 / 2

اذا عالج ذكره بيده حتى أمنى...عامة مشائخنا

استحسنو وأفتوا بالفساد. وفى الخلاصة:لا كفارة عليه [100]

The act in itself is Makrūh Taḥrīmī (prohibitively disliked) according to Hanafī research, as Allāmah ibn Humām ﷺ has stated in Fathul Qadeer. Imām Mālik ﷺ is of the opinion that it's Harām. Faqeeh Abul Layth Samarqandī ﷺ, who is a Hanafī, also classed it as Harām. [101]

The Daleel (proof) for both opinions is in the Ayah:

وَالَّذِيْنَ هُمْ لِفُرُوْجِهِمْ حٰفِظُوْنَ ۞

اِلَّا عَلٰى اَزْوَاجِهِمْ اَوْ مَا مَلَكَتْ اَيْمَانُهُمْ فَاِنَّهُمْ غَيْرُ مَلُوْمِيْنَ ۞

فَمَنِ ابْتَغٰى وَرَآءَ ذٰلِكَ فَاُولٰٓئِكَ هُمُ الْعٰدُوْنَ ۞

"And who guard their private parts. Except from their wives or from those (bondwomen whom) they own, as they are not to be blamed. And whosoever seeks other than this, they are the ones who exceed the limits."
[102]

Masturbation is exceeding the limits. There is also a Hadīth narrated here:

نَاكِحُ الْيَدِ مَلْعُوْنٌ [103]

"One who derives pleasure with his own hands is Mal'oon (cursed)."

However, this is not proven to be a Hadīth of Rasūlullāh ﷺ. It is most likely the saying of someone from the Salaf, which was quoted as a Hadīth.

---

[100] تاتارخانية ص 0 / 2 الهندية ص 205 / 1 فتح القدير ونهاية ص 234 / 2 احكام ص 290

[101] تنبيه ص 358

[102] Qur'ān 23:5-7.

[103] كشف الخفاء ص 291 / 2

قال جريج سألت عطاء عنه فقال مكروه سمعت

ان قوما يحشرون وأيديهم حُبالى فأظن أنهم هؤلاَء [104]

Jurayj ﷺ says that he asked Ataa (ibn Abi Rabaah) ﷺ about it. He said, "It is disliked. I have heard that certain people will be resurrected on the Day of Judgement while their hands will be (swollen) like heavily pregnant (women). I think it is these people."

وعن سعيد ابن جبير قال عذب الله امة يعبثون بمذاكيرهم [105]

Saeed Ibn Jubair ﷺ says, "Allāh punished a nation who used to play with their genitals."

What if a woman masturbates by inserting something in her vagina to derive sexual pleasure? I could not find this Mas'ala in Fiqhi books. The principles of Fiqh state that if the inserted item was dry and it did not fully disappear i.e. part of it remained out, the fast would not break. However, if the object fully disappeared, or it had some gel on it or it was taken out with some discharge on it and then re-entered, then the fast will break. Qadhā will be necessary.

ولو ادخل اصبعه فى استه او المرأة فى فرجها لا يفسد. وهو المختار الا اذا كانت

مبتلّة بالماء او الدهن فحينئذ يفسد لوصول الماء او الدهن. هكذا فى الظهيرة [106]

"If someone inserted his finger in his anus, or a woman in her vagina, the fast will not break (according to the preferred opinion). However, if the finger was wet with water or oil, the fast will break, because the water and the oil reach inside."

---

[104] تنبيه الغافلين ص 358

[105] تنبيه الغافلين ص 359

[106] الفتاوى الهندية ص 204 / 1 احكام ص 295

Based on this, we can say her fast will break.

If a woman inserted some medicine into the vagina, the fast will break.

قال فى بحر الرائق "لأن الإقطار فى قبل

المرأة يفسد الصوم بلا خلاف على الصحيح [107]

In Ahsan ul Fatāwā it is written that if some cream is applied to the outer layer of the vagina, due to a rash, the fast would not break. The other is the inner part, which is round. If medicine is inserted there, or the cream reaches inside, the fast will break. [108]

If something was placed inside a woman's private part, it would break her fast. This is because in a woman's body, there is a natural passage which takes the substance inside, so her fast would be broken. [109]

VAGINAL EXAMINATION AND SMEAR TEST

A woman who attends for a smear test or vaginal examination whilst fasting. If the mechanical instrument used for the examination, or the hand (in the case of a manual examination) was dry, it would not break the fast. However, if there was some gel on it, or it was withdrawn and reinserted with some discharge on it, it will break the fast. [110] It would be safer not to have such tests during Ramadhān.

Some ladies ask if Ghusl becomes Fardh after a smear test. The answer is no. Ghusl only becomes Fardh upon sexual intercourse or the ejaculation of semen. Neither takes place here, so Ghusl will not become Fardh. However, Wudhū will break because of the discharge that comes out.

If a woman was raped during her fast (Allāh forbid!) or intercourse was forced upon her whilst she was sleeping or unconscious, her fast will break.

---

[107] البحر الرائق ص 488 / 2 تحفة ص 71

[108] Ahsan ul Fatāwā Pg.438/4. Masā'il Raf'at Qasimi Pg.114.

[109] Jadeed Fiqhi Masā'il Pg.97.

[110] تحفة ص 71

She will only have to keep Qadhā. The other person will have to keep Qadhā and give Kaffārah as well.

وان كانت مكرهة فعليها القضاء دون الكفارة

وكذا اذا كانت مكرهة فى الإبتداء ثم طاوعته بعد ذلك ١١١

If someone touched the body of another person, was aroused, and as a result ejaculated, the fast will break. Only Qadhā will be necessary. If ejaculation did not take place, the fast will not break. [112]

If one was sitting with his wife and ejaculated just by looking at her, (this happens due to weakness, medical attention should be sought), the fast will not break, as there was no touching involved. Similar will be the case of looking at a non-Mahram and releasing semen without touching, masturbation etc.

If a husband inserted his finger in the wife's vagina, his fast will not break. With regards to her fast, there is some detail. If the finger was wet at the time of inserting, or it was dry but he extracted it and then reinserted it, then the wife's fast will break. She will have to keep Qadhā, but Kaffārah will not be necessary. [113]

If a husband inserted his finger in the vagina of the wife to apply some medicine, then they were aroused by sexual desire, they thought their fast was broken so they had intercourse, their fast will be broken, and they will both have to keep Qadhā. As for the Kaffārah, the husband will have to give Kaffārah, not the wife. This is because her fast was already broken by the insertion of the medicine, and then the intercourse took place.

If two women were to derive sexual pleasure with one another, (which is Harām) and they reached a state of orgasm, their fast will be broken. They will have to keep Qadhā, but Kaffārah will not be Fardh upon them. If they did not reach the state of orgasm, the fast will not break. [114]

---

[111] عالمجيرى ص 205 / 1 تحفة ص 71

[112] مسائل ص 80

[113] Ahsan ul Fatāwā 9447 Vol.4 / Masā'il Raf'at Pg.117.

[114] Hindiyyah Pg.20 Vol.2. Masā'il Pg.113.

INSERTING A CATHETER

If a man was having trouble passing water, and a catheter was inserted into the bladder, will his fast break? Imām Abū Hanīfā 🕮 and Imām Muhammad 🕮 are of the opinion that his fast will not break. This is because there is no direct passage [115] between the urethra and the stomach, therefore, the fast will not break. [116] However, if a woman was to insert some medicine in her vagina, her fast will break as there is a direct passage to her stomach. [117]

ANUS

If one uses Enema to empty the bowels, this will break the fast as it has a direct link to the digestive system.

واذا احتقن يفسد صومه [118]

If someone inserted a suppository into the anus or applied cream e.g. for piles, the fast will only break if the substance reached up to the place of 'Huqna' (up to the level of the rectum). This can only happen if the suppository is inserted with force and the effect can be felt inside, or the medicine travels slowly upwards. One should be careful and avoid it during the fast. Use it at night time if possible.

The same ruling will apply if a dry piece of cloth/tissue or something was inserted in such a way that it disappeared inside the body, the fast will break. If it did not totally disappear, part of it remained outside, the fast will not break. Where the fast breaks, only Qadhā will be necessary. Kaffārah will not apply. [119]

---

[115] منفذ أصل

[116] عالمجيرى ص 104 / 1.

[117] مشائل رفعة قاسمى ص 115 . جديد فقهى مسائل ص 97

[118] تاتارخانية ص 365 / 2 تحفة ص 71

[119] Masā'il Raf'at Qasimi Pg.81.

If someone had intercourse into the anus of a man or a woman, both parties' fast will break and Qadhā and Kaffārah will both be necessary. [120]

ثم عندنا كما تجب الكفارة بالوقاع على الرجل تجب على المرأة ـ

قوله "تجب على المرأة" لو قال على المفعول به كان أفيد [121]

Note: the act itself is Harām. It has been declared Harām in the Tawrāt, Zaboor, Injeel and the Qur'ān; all four religious books. The gravity of the sin increases if it is committed during the month of Ramadhān. Such people should seize the initiative of Ramadhān to do Taubah and repent wholeheartedly.

THE REST OF THE BODY

If someone had an open wound in the abdomen or the brain, and applied medicine, which went inside, the fast will be broken and a Qadhā will have to be kept.

وما وصل الى الجوف او الى الدماغ من المخارق الأصلية فسد الصوم [122]

If someone had an operation during Ramadhān, if nothing reached inside the stomach or the brain, the fast will be ok. However, if general anaesthetic was administered, then the medicine goes inside. Therefore, the fast will break.

If someone went for dialysis during Ramadhān, then one has to remember that this only cleans the blood, flushes the kidneys and nothing reaches the stomach or the brain. Therefore, dialysis itself will not break the fast.

---

[120] احكام ص 298

[121] الهداية و فتح القدير ص 342 / 2

[122] بدائع الصنائع ص 606 / 2

However, if one consumed some food or drink after dialysis, the fast will break. [123]

If the kidney patient struggles to fast on the day of dialysis, he could leave that day's fast and fast on the other days. Then, when Ramadhān finishes, he could make up for the days missed. If he was old and so ill that he was unable to make up for the missed ones, he could give Fidyā.

CUPPING, BLOODLETTING AND INJECTIONS

If a person injects something in the body through the veins, or takes blood out for testing diabetes or has Hijāmah (cupping) done on him, in all cases the fast will not break according to the Hanafī research.

Note: Some people say that cupping breaks the fast. They take the Daleel from the Hadīth:

"أفطر الحاجم والمحجوم"

"The cupper and the cupped one have both broken their fast." [124]

Rasūlullāh ﷺ made the above remark when he saw a person cupping another person in Ramadhān while both were fasting.

The Hanafīyah put forward another Hadīth:

ثلاث لا يفطرن الصائم الحجامة والقيء والاحتلام [125]

"Three things do not break the fast. Cupping, vomit and (having a) wet dream." [126]

To reconcile between both Ahādīth, the Hanafīyah say that in the second Hadīth, Rasūlullāh ﷺ is mentioning a general rule. Whereas in the first, he meant to say that they are very close to breaking their fast. Such phrases are normal in the Arabic language.

---

[123] أحكام ص 239

[124] Abū Dāwūd.

[125] رواه أحمد والترمذى

[126] Tirmīdhī, Ahmad.

In order to understand this, we have to look at how they used to cup in those days. They would have a horn of a bull. The sharp end would have a hole, through which the cupper would suck very hard. There was a risk that some blood could end up in his mouth and if he swallowed it, his fast would break.

As for the cupped person, if he fainted or too much blood was extracted, and he became so weak that he had to eat or drink something, his fast would break. This is why Rasūlullāh 🕮 meant to say, "They are very close to breaking their fasts."

INJECTIONS

Hadhrat Muftī Shafī Sahib 🕮 has written a detailed Fatwā with regards to injections. The Fatwā was then attested, by the likes of Hadhrat Maulānā Hussain Ahmed Madanī 🕮 and Hadhrat Maulānā Ashraf Alī Thānwī 🕮. The reality is that whatever is inserted into the body through injection, travels through the veins before it reaches the heart, brain or stomach. The passage it travels through is not taken as a direct one. [127]

Many examples can be found for this, in the work of the Fuqahā, where they deduce that the fast is not broken when something does not reach inside directly.

They say that injury is of two types:

[1] Aammah [آمّة]
[2] Jaa'ifah [جائفة]

Aammah is a deep injury, which reaches the roots of the brain. When medicine is applied, it goes inside directly. Jaa'ifah is a deep injury that affects the abdomen. Any medicine administered there, reaches the stomach. Since they both reach inside directly, they break the fast.

As for the other injuries like on the thigh, shin, arm etc. any medicine applied there doesn't reach the stomach directly. Even though the effects can

---

[127] منفذ اصلى

reach the stomach at some level, the Fuqahā state that this does not invalidate the fast. [128]

Muftī Shafī Sahib ﷺ writes, it is very clear that injections did not exist in the time of Rasūlullāh ﷺ nor during the times of the A'imā Mujtahideen. Therefore, no one can produce a Hadīth or any quote of the A'imā with regards to the injection Mas'ala. We will have to analyse it with some general principles and similarities.

We can take the Mas'ala from a snake or scorpion bite. The venom penetrates into the body. Most times, snake poison affects the brain and kills. Wasp bites swell the part which was bitten, which means that some foreign body has entered inside. However, no Faqeeh in the world has said that this invalidates the fast. They all say that it should be treated, but the fast will be ok, as long as nothing is consumed orally to treat the bite.

Injections were only invented after experiencing the effects of insect bites. i.e. that the bites had an immediate effect on the body, so injections should also work in the same way, in the sense that the medicine would immediately affect the body, rather than traveling through the stomach and blood system which would require some time.

When we carefully study the wordings of Badaa'ius Sanaa'i regarding the reasons snake and insect bites don't break the fast, we understand that when something enters the human body, it does not instantly break the fast. There are two conditions attached to it:

[1] It should reach the inside of the stomach or into the brain.

[2] It should reach there through a direct passage. [129] (This is why if a stroke patient has a tube inserted into his throat and liquid food goes directly to his stomach, it invalidates the fast).

With the case of an injection, no doubt the effects reach the whole body, however, this is not through منفذ أصل (a direct, original passage). We see in

---

[128] Masā'il Pg.136. Hidāyah Pg.200.

[129] منفذ أصل

hot seasons people bathe with cold water. The cold effects go inside the body and cool it down just as a chilled drink would cool it. However, this coolness goes through the pores of the skin and not directly to the inside (jawf).

الجواب صحیح مولانا اشرف علی تھانوی، مولانا حسین احمد مدنی، مولانا اصغر حسین، مولانا اعزاز علی

11 ربیع الاول 1350ھ. مسائل روزہ مولانا رفعت قاسمی ص 139، 138، 137

ترجمۃ شیخ عبد الرحیم

Similarly, injections take the medicine, glucose, penicillin, insulin etc. through the veins. Glucose energises the body but just energising does not break the fast. Therefore, the conclusion is that injections do not break the fast, unless an injection is administered directly in the stomach or in the brain.

Please note that it would be Makrūh to take glucose injections during the fast because it contradicts the purpose of fasting. Also, it would be preferable to take all injections after Iftaar, during the night. This is because there is some Ikhtilāf (difference of opinion) in the Mas'ala, so Ihtiyāt (caution) would be better. [130]

ACUPUNCTURE

If someone has acupuncture while fasting, his fast will not break. This is because it only affects the skin. Nothing goes into the stomach.

ENDOSCOPY

If a camera was inserted into the back passage for an internal investigation, it would not break the fast if it was dry. However, they normally apply some gel to ease the insertion. In that case, the fast does break. [131]

---

[130] أحكام

[131] أحكام ص 250

ANGIOGRAPHY

In an angiography, a dye which shows up on x-ray is introduced into the blood stream. The principals of Fiqh support that it should not break the fast, as nothing directly reaches the digestive system. However, if medication has to be used, it is better to avoid it during the fasting days, unless it is extremely necessary to save one's life.

LAPAROSCOPY

An instrument is inserted through a small incision in the abdomen to examine the abdominal cavity, or to perform operations. Since it enters the abdomen and normally lubricant is applied to the instrument, the fast will break.

Taking biopsies or samples from the liver or the other organs does not break the fast – as long as this is not accompanied by the administration of solutions or other substances. Maulānā Khālid Saifullāh [Dāmat Barakātuhum] analyses it with a Mas'ala mentioned by Ibn Nujaym ﷺ, that if a person was to tie a piece of meat with a string and lower it down the throat and then pull it back out, this would not break the fast.

ولو شد الطعام بخيط وأرسله فى حلقه وطرف الخيط فى يده لا يفسد الصوم [132]

GASTROSCOPY

This does not break the fast, provided it is not accompanied by the administration of solutions or other substances. However, gastroscopy always needs a local anaesthetic spray for the back of the throat and if this is swallowed, which in nearly all cases it is, then the fast will be broken.

ENDOSCOPY

This could be via mouth which is called gastroscopy or via the anus which is called colonoscopy or sigmoidoscopy. It would normally break the fast.

---

[132] البحر الرائق ص 279 / 2 جديد فقهى مسائل ص 126

NICOTINE PATCHES

If a smoker uses nicotine patches, the fast will not break. This is clear, because they are applied to the skin and there is no direct penetration to the stomach or the brain.

Note: Consult a Muslim physician before taking any of the above tests whilst fasting. If the advice given is that the test is absolutely necessary, then it should take precedence over the fast. If they are not necessary, delay them until after Ramadhān.

KAFFĀRAH

When a fast is deliberately broken, Kaffārah becomes necessary. Kaffārah is to make Qadhā of the broken fast and then fast for two months continuously, without any break in the middle. If one missed a day, he would have to start the two months from the beginning. If one cannot fast, he may feed 60 Masakeen (poor people) or free one slave.

Some Ulamā (the Salafī scholars) say Kaffārah only becomes necessary by deliberate sexual intercourse. However, the majority of the Ulamā and the Hanafī scholars say that it becomes Wājib by eating or drinking deliberately (without genuine necessity) as well.

If someone broke a few fasts in Ramadhān, does he have to give Kaffārah for every broken fast, or can there be 'Tadakhul' (combining them into one)?

The Salafī scholars say that Kaffārah will have to be given separately for each broken fast. So if one broke five fasts, he will have to give five Kaffārah.

The Hanafī scholars say there will be 'Tadakhul' in Kaffārah. Then, there are three opinions of the Muftiyāne Kirām:

[1] There can be Tadakhul of Kaffārah for one Ramadhān, not two separate ones. [133]

[2] In *Behisti Gohar* it says Tadakhul can be of separate Ramadhān's as well.

---

[133] Behisti Zewar.

[3] In *Ahsan ul Fatāwā* it says that if Kaffārah was due to sexual intercourse, Tadakhul can be for one Ramadhān only. However, if it was due to eating or drinking, Tadakhul can be for various Ramadhāns as well.

[By Sūfī Muftī Tāhir Hafizahullāh]

SALĀHTUT TARĀWĪH

One of the unique features and beauty of Ramadhān is the Salāh of Tarāwīh. It increases the Noor of Ramadhān. It also increases in our hearts, the desire for worship.

It is narrated in Sahīh Ahādīth, that Rasūlullāh ﷺ led the Sahāba in a special Salāh for three nights during Ramadhān. However, observing the great zeal of the Sahāba and their arrival in huge numbers, Rasūlullāh ﷺ stopped this practice. He did not come out of his I'tikāf area and into the Masjid. He then remarked in the morning, "I knew of your presence. What stopped me from leading you was that I feared it would be made compulsory upon you." [134]

Rasūlullāh ﷺ continued to urge the Sahāba to perform extra worship during Ramadhān, e.g. his saying, "One Nafl of Ramadhān is equal to one Fardh in other months, and one Fardh is equal to seventy Fardh in other months." [135]

He also said, "Whoever stands in prayer at night during Ramadhān with faith and sincerity, will have his sins forgiven." [136]

He praised some Sahāba who were praying in congregation behind Ubayy ibn Ka'b ﷺ. [137]

This shows that this special prayer, which we name 'Tarāwīh', does have some basis from the prophetic era. Then, in the Siddīqī era and the early Fārūqī era, matters remained the same, i.e. people would pray behind various Huffāz of the Qur'ān. It was in Ramadhān 14 AH, that Sayyidunā Umar Farooq

---

[134] Bukhārī Vol.1 pg.269.
[135] Ibn Khuzaimah.
[136] Bukhārī Vol.1 pg.269.
[137] Bayhaqī Vol.2 pg.697.

saw people in small groups behind various Ḥuffāẓ, that he thought, "If I were to gather these behind one Imām, it would be more beneficial." He did have evidence from the practice of Rasūlullāh 🌸, and since Rasūlullāh 🌸 had departed from this world, there was no risk of it being made Fardh, so he got them all together behind one Hāfiz.

He instructed Ubay ibn Kaʿb 🌸 to lead the people with twenty rakʿāts. Some narrations state that they would pray eight with three witr. However, most riwāyāt state twenty. It is possible that they started with eight, however, since the rakʿāts were lengthy, standing was prolonged and hard, Sayyidunā Umar 🌸 instructed them to read twenty, so the rakʿāts were shortened and standing was eased.

Abdul Azīz ibn Rufay 🌸 says, "Ubay Ibn Kaʿb 🌸 would lead people in Ramadhān with twenty rakʿāts of Tarāwīh, then he would finish with three rakʿāts of witr. [138]

Saaʾib Ibn Yazeed 🌸 reports that the Sahāba would stand in Ramadhān with twenty rakʿāts during the time of Umar 🌸 and during the era of Uthmān 🌸. [139]

Yazeed Ibn Roomaan 🌸 says, "People would pray twenty-three rakʿāts in Ramadhān Mubārak during the Khilāfah of Umar ibn Khattab 🌸. [140]

Abū Abdul Rahman Sulami 🌸 says, "Alī 🌸 called upon the Ḥuffāẓ and picked from them some who could lead people with twenty rakʿāts of Tarāwīh. Then Alī 🌸 would lead them in Witr. [141]

One Dhaeef narration from Ibn Abbās 🌸 states that it was the practice of Rasūlullāh 🌸 to pray twenty rakʿāts in Ramadhān. [142]

Due to the above narrations, the majority of scholars of the Ummah and all of the four great Imams (Abū Hanīfā, Shāfiʾī, Ahmad and Mālik) unanimously declare that Tarāwīh is nothing less than twenty. (Imām Mālik has said in one Qawl (narration) that it is thirty-six). Twenty has been the practice in

---

[138] Ibn Abī Shaybah pg.165 v.2.
[139] Bayhaqi in as Sunan al Kubra pg.699 V.1.
[140] Ibid.
[141] Ibid.
[142] Ibn Abī Shaybah pg.166 V.2, Bayhaqi pg.698 V.2.

Haramayn Shareefayn for the last 1400 years. The correct amount of Tarāwīh rak'āts is twenty; hence, one should always pray twenty rak'āts.

Some people say it is eight rak'āts and they bring forth the Hadīth of Ā'isha ❀. However, this is not correct. She is talking about Tahajjud. Tarāwīh and Tahajjud are both totally different Salāhs. One is early in the night whereas the other is in the latter part of the night. She has clearly stated the words, "In Ramadhān and in other months." Only Tahajjud is prayed in the other eleven months.

SOME MASĀ'IL OF TARĀWĪH

The Shar'iī ruling for Tarāwīh: It is Sunnah Muakkadah to pray twenty rak'āts of Tarāwīh in units of two at a time, for men and for women.

التراويح سنة مؤكدة لمواظبة الخلفاء الراشدين للرجال والنساء اجماعا ¹⁴³

REASON FOR NAMING IT TARĀWĪH

Tarāwīh is the plural of Tarwīhah. Tarwīh is from 'Raahah' which means to take a short rest. Since they would pray four rak'āts and then then relax a bit and then another four and so forth, it was given the name Tarāwīh. The name might be new, but the actual Salāh is not new.

TIME OF TARĀWĪH

The time of Tarāwīh is after performing Ishā until Subhe Sadiq. It is not allowed to pray Tarāwīh before Ishā. If someone was late, Ishā had finished and Tarāwīh had started, he must pray Ishā first and then join Tarāwīh. He can't join in the Tarāwīh and say that he will pray Ishā later on.

Witr should be prayed after Tarāwīh. However, if it was prayed after Ishā and before Tarāwīh, it would still be correct.

ووقتها بعد صلاة العشاء إلى الفجر قبل الوتر وبعده على الاصح ¹⁴⁴

در مختار ص 429 / 2 طحطاوى على المراقى ¹⁴³

در مختار ص 430 / 2 ¹⁴⁴

TARĀWĪH IN CONGREGATION

It is Sunnah Alal Kifāyah to perform Tarāwīh in congregation in the Masjid of the local area. If there is no Tarāwīh Jamā'ah in an area, the whole area will be sinful.

$$\text{والجماعة فيها سنة على الكفاية فى الأصح فلو تركها اهل المسجد أثموا}^{145}$$

INTENTION IN TARĀWĪH

Tarāwīh and the rest of the Sunnahs and Nawāfil can be performed with the simple intention of Salāh. They don't need to be specified. However, caution is in specifying Tarāwīh as Tarāwīh when making intention.

$$(\text{وَكَفَى مُطْلَقُ نِيَّةِ الصَّلَاةِ}) \text{وَإِنْ لَمْ يَقُلْ لِلّهِ}(\text{لِنَفْلٍ وَسُنَّةٍ}) \text{رَاتِبَةٍ}$$

$$(\text{وَتَرَاوِيحَ}) \text{عَلَى الْمُعْتَمَدِ، إِذْ تَعْيِينُهَا بِوُقُوعِهَا وَقْتَ الشُّرُوعِ، وَالتَّعْيِينُ أَحْوَطُ}^{146}$$

KHATM OF QUR'ĀN

Completing one Qur'ān in Tarāwīh is Sunnah. More than once is Mustahabb, desirable.

$$(\text{وَالْخَتْمُ}) \text{مَرَّةً سُنَّةٌ وَمَرَّتَيْنِ فَضِيلَةٌ وَثَلَاثًا أَفْضَلُ.}^{147}$$

KHATM OF QUR'ĀN IN TARĀWĪH

It is Sunnah to complete one Khatm during Tarāwīh. [148]

One may ask, "How can Tarāwīh and Khatm it be classed as Sunnah?" The answer is that Sunnah is that act which was practiced upon with punctuality

---

[145] در مختار ص 431 / 2 عالمجيرى ص 117 / 1

[146] در مختار ص 82 / 2

[147] در مختار ص 433 / 2 عالمجيرى ص 117 / 1

[148] Durr Mukhtar with Shāmī pg.433 V.2.

by either Rasūlullāh ﷺ or by the rightly guided Khulafā e Kiraam. One Hadīth says:

$$عَلَيْكُمْ بِسُنَّتِيْ، وَسُنَّةِ الْخُلَفَاءِ الرَّاشِدِيْنَ الْمَهْدِيِّيْنَ، عَضُّوا عَلَيْهَا بِالنَّوَاجِذِ ^{149}$$

"Hold on to my Sunnah and the Sunnah of the rightly guided Khulafā. Bite on to them with your molar teeth." [150]

He didn't say, "Hold on to my Hadīth." So we shouldn't restrict Dalaa'il with Hadīth, by demanding a Hadīth for everything. We have to look at the general Sunnah. He also said:

$$"اقتدوا باللذين من بعدى من اصحابى ابى بكر وعمر"$$

"Follow my two companions after me, Abū Bakr and Umar."

And:

$$"ان الله جعل الحق على لسان عمر وقلبه"$$

"Allāh has placed Haq upon the heart of Umar ﷺ and his tongue."

He also said that Umar is 'Muhaddath' i.e. 'Mulham', the inspired one. He also said, "If there was to be a prophet after me, it would be Umar ﷺ."

May Allāh ﷺ reward Hadhrat Umar ﷺ who put so much emphasis on completing the Qur'ān that he preserved the Qur'ān by Tarāwīh.

Shaykh Abdul Qādir Jilānī ﷺ narrates in 'Ghunya' that during the Khilāfah of Alī ﷺ, he once passed by a Masjid on the 1st of Ramadhān. He heard the sound of Tilāwah in Tarāwīh. He remarked,

$$"نوّر الله قبر عمر كما نوّر مساجد الله بالقران"$$

"May Allāh fill Umar's ﷺ grave with light just as he

---

[149] ابن ماجه

[150] Ibn Mājah.

filled the Masājid with the Noor of Qur'ān!" [151]

The reality is that if there was no Tarāwīh, many Ḥuffāẓ would have forgotten their Qur'ān. Since they have to lead in Tarāwīh, they memorise and go over it every year. In this way, the Qur'ān will remain protected until the Day of Qiyāmah.

Allāh ﷻ chose Umar ؓ to initiate the Sunnah of Tarāwīh in the present manner. Then Uthmān ؓ and Alī ؓ confirmed it. Not only that, all the Sahābā (who were of the best generation) agreed to it. Allāh's ﷻ hand is upon the Jamā'ah. The Ummah can never collaborate upon error. So, the twenty rak'āts and Khatm of Qur'ān is the proper Sunnah.

If someone leaves after eight rak'āts, he misses out not on two, in fact three Sunnah's:

[1] The Sunnah of performing twenty rak'āts.

[2] The Sunnah of listening to the whole Qur'ān.

[3] The Sunnah of performing Witr with Jamā'ah, during Ramadhān. Therefore, we should pray full twenty rak'āts Tarāwīh.

Many Masājid have eight Rak'āts only Tarāwīh. In some Masājid, people leave after eight Rak'āts. They go home and watch T.V. until late at night. Many keep gossiping in the parking lodge while those who pray 20 finish and come out. This is all Mahroomi, deprivation. May Allāh ﷻ guide the Ummah.

TWO TARĀWĪH CONGREGATIONS IN ONE MASJID

It would be Makrūh (disliked) to do Jamā'at twice in one Masjid, on one Imām Musallāh.

$$\text{"ولو صلى التراويح مرتين فى مسجد يكره"}$$

غنيمة الطالبين ص 427 [151]

LADIES JAMA'AH OF TARĀWĪH

If ladies were to join in with men in Tarāwīh, there would be no harm. However, if ladies made their own Jamā'ah with a lady Imām, it would be Makrūh. If they did so, their Imām should not stand ahead of the Saff (row), she should stand in the middle.

قال محمد لا يعجبنا أن تؤم المرأة فان فعلت قامت فى وسط

الصف مع النساء كما فعلت عائشة وهو قول ابى حنيفة الخ. ¹⁵²

A HĀFIZ LEADING WOMEN ONLY [WITH NO OTHER MEN BEHIND HIM]

If a Hāfiz led only women in Tarāwīh, it would be necessary to have a Mahram relative, of the Imām or his wife among the ladies. Otherwise, it would be Makrūh to lead women only.

ويكره حضورهن الجماعة مطلق على المذهب كما تكره امامة

الرجل لهن فى بيت ليس معهن رجل غيره ولا محرم منه او زوجته ¹⁵³

PRAYING TARĀWĪH IN UNITS OF FOUR

If Tarāwīh was prayed in units of four, would it be ok? If one prayed four rak'āts and sat in the middle for Tashahhud, it would be ok. However, if he did not sit in the second Rak'ah, and prayed four all together, the first two rak'āts will be void. Only the last two will be correct. Therefore, whatever Qur'ān was recited in the first two rak'āts will have to be repeated. [154]

The preferred method is to read in twos.

---

¹⁵² كتاب الآثار ص 603 / 1

¹⁵³ شامى ص 307 / 2 تحفة ص 86

¹⁵⁴ تحفة ص 86

RESTING AFTER EACH FOUR UNITS OF TARĀWĪH

It is desirable to have a slight pause after every four rak'āts.

ويجلس ندبا بين كل أربعة بقدرها وكذا بين الخامسة والوتر ¹⁵⁵

What should one read in the Tarweehah (the pause after four rak'āts)? There is no special Dhikr to be made during the Waqfa (pause) between every four rak'āts. One has a choice of doing whatever Dhikr comes to his mind. One could recite some Qur'ān, Tasbeeh, Istighfār, Salāt 'Alan Nabī ﷺ etc.

Some Fuqahā have mentioned the following Tasbeeh which one may pray if he wishes:

سُبْحَانَ ذِي الْمُلْكِ وَالْمَلَكُوْتِ، سُبْحَانَ ذِي الْعِزَّةِ وَالْعَظَمَةِ وَالْقُدْرَةِ وَالْكِبْرِيَاءِ وَالْجَبَرُوْتِ، سُبْحَانَ الْمَلِكِ الْحَيِّ الَّذِيْ لَا يَمُوْتُ، سُبُّوْحٌ قُدُّوْسٌ رَبُّ الْمَلَائِكَةِ وَالرُّوْحِ، لَا إِلَهَ إِلاَّ اللهُ نَسْتَغْفِرُ اللهَ، نَسْأَلُكَ الْجَنَّةَ وَنَعُوْذُ بِكَ مِنَ النَّارِ ¹⁵⁶

WITR WITH JAMĀ'AH AFTER TARĀWĪH

It is more virtuous to perform Witr Salāh with Jamā'ah after having performed the Tarāwīh. This is what Sayyidunā Umar ﷺ instructed Sayyidunā Ubay ibn Ka'b ﷺ to do. The Sahāba practiced on it and it has been the practice of the Salaf-e-Sālihīn ever since.

وفيه اى رمضان يصلى الوتر وقيامه بها ¹⁵⁷

QADHĀ OF TARĀWĪH

If someone missed Tarāwīh altogether and the time of Ishā also lapsed, there is no Qadhā for Tarāwīh. This is because Tarāwīh is not Fardh, its only Nafl

¹⁵⁵ در مختار ص 433 / 2

¹⁵⁶ شامى ص 433 / 2 تحفة ص 87

¹⁵⁷ در مختار ص 437 / 2

(i.e. Sunnah Muakkadah). If someone missed many years of Tarāwīh, he would not have to make up for them.

وَلَا تُقْضَى إِذَا فَاتَتْ أَصْلًا وَلَا وَحْدَهُ فِي الْأَصَحِّ

فَإِنْ قَضَاهَا كَانَتْ نَفْلًا مُسْتَحَبًّا وَلَيْسَ بِتَرَاوُحٍ [158]

ZAKĀH

Zakāh is one of the five pillars of Islam, i.e. it is from the fundamentals of our religion. Giving in charity is a practice widely encouraged in Islam and as such, Shariah has made it necessary upon us to dispense a small amount of our wealth each year for the poor and needy. When a person's wealth reaches a certain amount, his wealth will be zakatable, i.e. he must pay Zakāh (alms/obligatory charity) on it. Sharī'ah does not like to overburden us, so we are only required to pay 2.5% (one fortieth) of our zakatable wealth.

Due to the increased rewards for giving charity in the month of Ramadhān, many people take the opportunity to give their Zakāh in this month. Therefore, we decided to mention a few points regarding Zakāh here.

There are many virtues recorded in the Ahādīth for giving Zakāh. In Hajjatul Wada, Rasūlullāh ﷺ said:

فَقَالَ رَسُولُ الله صَلَّى اللهُ عَلَيْهِ وَسَلَّمَ : اعْبُدُوْا رَبَّكُمْ، وَصَلُّوا خَمْسَكُمْ، وَصُوْمُوا شَهْرَكُمْ، وَأَدُّوا زَكَاةَ أَمْوَالِكُمْ، وَأَطِيعُوْا ذَا أَمْرِكُمْ؛ تَدْخُلُوْا جَنَّةَ رَبِّكُمْ ـ

"Rasūlullāh ﷺ said, "Worship your lord, pray your five (daily prayers), fast your month (of Ramadhān), give the Zakāh from your wealth and obey the commands of your leaders, you will enter the Jannah of your Rabb." [159]

---

[158] در مختار ص 431 / 2

[159] Ahmad.

In another place Rasūlullāh ﷺ said:

دَاوُوا مَرْضَاكُمْ بِالصَّدَقَةِ، وَحَصِّنُوْا أَمْوَالَكُمْ بِالزَّكَاةِ ـ

"Cure your sick ones by (giving) charity and
protect your wealth by (paying) Zakāh." [160]

As for those who refuse to pay Zakāh, or those who are lazy and negligent when it comes to giving Zakāh, they should be mindful of the severe warnings found in the Ahādīth. In one place, Rasūlullāh ﷺ mentioned:

من أتاه الله مالا فلم يؤد زكوته مُثِّل له ماله يوم القيامة شجاعا اقرع له زبيبتان

يطوقه يوم القيامة ثم يأخذ بلهزمتيه يعني شدقيه ثم يقول انا مالك انا كنزك ثم

قرا ولا يحسبن اللذين يبخلون بما اتاهم الله من فضله هو خيرا لهم بل هو شر

لهم سيطوقون ما بخلوا به يوم القيامة ـ

"Whoever Allāh has given wealth but doesn't pay Zakāh, his wealth will be transformed on the Day of Judgement into a serpent, bald (due to its toxic venom), with two black spots above its eyes. It will be wrapped around his neck (like a collar) on the Day of Judgement, then the serpent will take hold of him by his cheeks and say, "I am your wealth, I am your (acquired) treasure." Then Rasūlullāh ﷺ recited, "Those who withhold in miserliness what Allāh has given them out of His grace should not take it as good for them. Instead, it is bad for them. They shall be forced, on the Doomsday, to put on what they withheld, as iron-collars round their necks." [161]

NOTE

The next ten [10] or so pages which contain the Masā'il of Zakāh, I'tikāf, Eid-ul-Fitr and Sadaqatul Fitr are all taken from a booklet which our Hazrat

---

[160] Bayhaqi in Shu'abul Imaan.
[161] Bukhārī.

Maulānā Yūsuf Motālā Sahib Nawwarallāhū Marqadahū had prepared to give out to students before they used to leave for the Ramadhān holidays.

Hazrat has compiled them in an extremely beautiful and succinct manner. This is the beauty of the writings of our Akābir.

Some editing was done by our respected Maulānā Zayd Mehtar Hafizahullāh. The Zakat calculation table was also added by Maulānā Zayd.

THE REQUIRED MINIMUM [NISĀB] FOR ONE TO BE LIABLE FOR ZAKĀH

If a person possesses 612.35 grams of silver or 87.479 grams of gold or any currency that equals the value of this amount of gold or silver, and this wealth remains in his possession for a complete year, then on the expiry of this year it will be Wājib on him to give Zakāh for it. However, if his wealth is less than this, Zakāh will not be Wājib. This amount is known as 'Nisāb'. (The grams are taken from the Hadīth of five Uqiya of silver and five Mithqāl of gold).

If a person possesses the Nisāb, i.e. the required minimum (of silver and gold) at the beginning and at the end of the year, Zakāh will be Wājib on him. If his wealth decreased during the course of the year below the level of Nisāb, one will not be absolved of giving one's Zakāh. However, if his entire wealth was destroyed, he won't be responsible for it, because he himself has become a Mustahiq (viable recipient) of Zakāh.

Note: If someone didn't know the end of his Zakāh year (from the day one became the owner of Nisāb) it may be advisable to take the opportunity of Ramadhān and dispense his Zakāh every year in Ramadhān. One has to keep a fixed date for Zakāh and calculate exactly on that date every year.

CONSIDERING DEBTS WHEN CALCULATING ZAKĀH

If a person is in debt, and his debts are equal or more to the total wealth he owns, he will be absolved from paying Zakāh. However, if his debts amassed to less than his overall wealth, then he must subtract the amount he owes from his wealth. Then, if what remains is equal to or more than Nisāb, he must pay Zakāh on that amount.

We often find that people owe thousands upon thousands of pounds due to mortgaging their houses or purchasing cars on finance. First of all, this is Harām. We should not waste our hard-earned wealth in paying interest, while incurring sin at the same time, a major sin.

However, many people ask, if the overall debt is more than the wealth they currently have, will this type of debt be considered when calculating Zakāh? For e.g. If Zayd had £15,000 in the bank but he owed £15,000 over three years due to financing his vehicle, would he still have to pay Zakāh? The answer is that the full amount owed will not be considered at the time of calculating Zakāh. Rather, the amount owed for that month will be subtracted from the full wealth, so, if for example Zayd owed £500 a month, when he calculates his Zakāh, he will subtract £500 from whatever he has in the bank. Thereafter, if what remains reaches the value of Nisāb, he must pay Zakāh on it, i.e. £14,500 in this case.

If someone lent another person money, he will still have to include that amount as part of his wealth when calculating Zakāh. For example, if Zayd lent 10k to an institute, he will have to pay Zakāh on it, even if that amount stays with the borrower for many years. Zayd will have to pay its Zakāh every year. However, if he no longer had any hope of receiving this money back, he will not have to pay Zakāh on it. For example, if the borrower filed for bankruptcy, he will no longer have the means to pay him, thus, one would not count such a loan as part of his wealth when calculating Zakāh.

UPON WHAT IS ZAKĀH OBLIGATORY ?

Zakāh is Wājib on all items of wealth, such as jewellery, utensils and ornaments etc. that have been made with gold or silver. This is irrespective of whether these items are in use or not. In other words, Zakāh is Wājib on everything that is made of gold or silver. However, if the combined value of all these items are less than the Nisāb, Zakāh will not be Wājib.

If the gold or silver is not pure but has been mixed with another metal, then one will have to check as to which is more in content. If the gold or silver is more, then the rules which are applicable to both will apply here as well. That is, if they equal the Nisāb, Zakāh will be Wājib. If the content of the other metal is more than that of the gold or silver, it will NOT be regarded as gold or silver.

A person does not have the complete Nisāb of gold nor of silver. Instead, he has a bit of gold and a bit of silver. If both are added together and their value equals the Nisāb of gold or silver, Zakāh will be Wājib. But if they do not equal the Nisāb of either gold or silver after adding them together, Zakāh will not be Wājib. If he has any other Zakatable assets, e.g. cash, shares etc, they will of course be added to the gold and silver.

If a person had money equal to the Nisāb, which was over and above his needs, and then before his zakatable year was over, he received an additional amount. This additional amount will not be calculated separately. Instead, it will be added to the original amount and upon the expiry of the year, Zakāh will be Wājib on the entire amount and it will be regarded as if the original amount and the additional amount was in his possession for one full year. For example, if a person sold his house and got £100,000 in his possession one week before Ramadhān (or the due date), he will have to give Zakāh on the whole amount, even if he was intending to purchase another property with that money. If it came to his possession one week after the calculation date, one will not have to include it. This is because he has already calculated and given his Zakāh. If that amount remains with him until the following year, he will have to pay it at that time.

Zakāh is not Wājib on household items such as utensils, pots, big pots, trays, basins, crockery and glassware, the house in which one lives, the clothes which one wears, jewellery made of pearls, etc. This is irrespective of the amount and irrespective of whether they are being used daily or not. However, if they are kept for the purpose of trade, Zakāh will be Wājib on them as well. In short, Zakāh is not Wājib on all items apart from gold and silver if they are not for the purpose of trade. But if they are for trade, Zakāh will be Wājib on them as well. For example, where a person has a business of cutlery, utensils, washing machines, cookers, fridges etc.

If a person owns several homes from which he collects rent. Zakāh is not Wājib on these homes irrespective of their value. Similarly, if a person purchases some utensils and hires them out, Zakāh will not be Wājib on these utensils. In short, by hiring or renting something out, Zakāh does not become Wājib on that thing. However, Zakāh will be Wājib on the rent accumulated at the end of the year. For example, if one accumulated £10,000 rent throughout the year, one will have to give zakat on £10,000.

WHO CAN RECEIVE ZAKĀH?

The person who has very little wealth or has no wealth at all to the extent that he does not have sufficient food for one day is regarded as a poor person. It is permissible to give Zakāh to such a person. It is also permissible for him to accept Zakāh money.

The person who possesses the Nisāb of either gold or silver, or trade goods which equal the Nisāb of either gold or silver is regarded as a rich person in the Sharī'ah. It is not permissible to give Zakāh money to him. Nor is it permissible for him to accept or consume Zakāh money.

The person who has belongings, which are not for trade/business but are over and above his basic needs, is also considered to be a rich person. It is not permissible to give Zakāh money to such a person as well. Although he is regarded as a rich person, Zakāh is not Wājib on him.

A person may not give Zakāh to one's parents, grandparents, great grandparents etc. nor one's children, grandchildren etc. Nor can a person give his Zakāh to his wife. However, it is allowed to give to one's brother, sister, aunt, uncle, cousin, in-laws etc.

It is not permissible to give one's Zakāh to build Masājid or madrassahs etc. similarly, it is not permissible to help with someone's funeral costs, because 'tamleek' (ownership) is necessary for Zakāh to be considered fulfilled. No one is the owner of the Masājid so one cannot give Zakāh money there, and a deceased person cannot become the owner of any property so Zakāh cannot be given there either.

Zakāh Calculation Table		
<u>Assets</u>		<u>Value in GBP</u>
Gold and Silver		
Value of Gold you possess		£
Value of Silver you possess		£
Cash		
Cash at home	Any currency acceptable in the market.	£
Cash in bank accounts	In any type of account	£
Money owed to you		£
Business Assets		
Shares & Stocks	Resale Value	£
Business Goods		£
Total:		£
<u>Liabilities</u>		<u>Value in GBP</u>
Money Owed (Borrowed or Credit)		£
Employees' Salaries		£
Other outgoings due (tax, rent, utilities).		£
Total:		£
Amount eligible for Zakāh:	i.e. Total assets minus liabilities = Amount on which Zakāh is payable	£
Amount you must pay for Zakāh:	i.e. Amount eligible for Zakāh x 0.025	£

I'TIKĀF

The practice of I'tikāf (remaining in seclusion) is a Sunnah that has remained in the Prophets throughout the ages. It is from the noble practices of Ibrāhīm 🕊 and many other prophets used to observe it. As stated in the Qur'ān, Hadhrat Mūsā 🕊 was also called to mount Toor for an I'tikāf of forty days, and even before receiving Prophethood, Rasūlullāh 🕊 used to spend a lot of time in seclusion in the cave of Hira. Therefore, after receiving Prophethood as well, Rasūlullāh 🕊 used to observe I'tikāf during the last ten days of Ramadhān on a regular basis.

Observing I'tikāf in the last ten days of Ramadhān is Sunnah Muakkadah Alal Kifāyah. i.e. an emphasised Sunnah, which is the duty of the whole community. If no one from the whole community observed I'tikāf in the last ten days of Ramadhān, the whole community will be sinful.

In order for the I'tikāf of a male to be valid, it must be done in a Masjid wherein at least the five daily prayers are prayed with congregation. As for a woman, she may reserve an area in the home as her place of I'tikāf. It is written is Shāmī that it is Makrūh Tanzīhī or Khilāf Awla (contrary to Sunnah) for a woman to go to the Masjid for I'tikāf. [162]

Although it is not permissible to leave the Masjid or place of I'tikāf unnecessarily, one may leave the Masjid to attend Jumu'ah (if it does not take place in the Masjid he is currently in) and to go to the toilet to relive himself or to go for a shower if he had a wet dream.

If there is no one to bring food to the Masjid, one may go home to eat. Similarly, a woman in her I'tikāf may go to the kitchen to prepare her food if there is no one to prepare it for her.

If someone did leave the Masjid unnecessarily, the I'tikāf will be broken, meaning that the Sunnah of the ten-day I'tikāf will not be fulfilled. Even though it would be best to stay in I'tikāf for the remaining days because he had originally made intention to stay for the full ten days, he would only need to do Qadhā (make up) of that day's I'tikāf. If he doesn't stay, he doesn't

---

[162] Shāmī Pg.441 V.2.

need to do Qadhā of the rest of the days that he missed, because each day of I'tikāf is counted separately.

It is not permissible to have sexual intercourse whilst in I'tikāf, and if one did so, whether it was on purpose or due to forgetfulness, the I'tikāf will be broken.

It is permissible for a businessman to conduct his business from the Masjid during I'tikāf, though he should not bring the actual goods into the Masjid. One may do his work on the computer, provided he does not disturb others and his work is minimized to necessity.

Some people are not able to observe the full ten days of I'tikāf, because they can't get that much time of work. They ask if they are allowed to go to work and then come back to the Masjid in the evening. In such a case, it will be permissible for a person to remain in I'tikāf, though it would not be counted as the Sunnah I'tikāf of ten days. Rather, it would be Nafl I'tikāf.

One should take the opportunity of I'tikāf and spend the time in worship; reciting Qur'ān, Nafl Salāh etc. If someone has missed many Salāh in the past, it is a good time to start making up for those missed prayers. It is usually very difficult to get a whole ten days just for worshipping Allāh ﷻ. Make use of the time and avoid pointless discussions and futile talk.

EID UL FITR

SOME RULES REGARDING EID UL FITR

[1] It is obligatory to offer a two Rak'ah prayer on the day of Eid ul Fitr to express gratitude to Allāh ﷻ.

[2] The time of Eid prayer begins when the sun rises one spear high (i.e. approx. 15 minutes after sunrise) and ends at its decline (i.e. noon).

[3] The Eid Khutbā after the Salāh is Sunnah. Listening to it is also Sunnah.

METHOD OF PRAYING EID SALĀH

One should firstly make Niyyah to offer two Rak'ah Wājib Eid ul Fitr Salāh, including six extra Takbīrs (saying Allāhu Akbar).

After the Niyyah, one should say the Takbīr Tahreemah (Allāhu Akbar), fold the hand and recite Thanā [... سُبْحَانَكَ اللَّهُمَّ]. Then say Allāhu Akbar thrice, each time raising the hands up to the ears and then dropping them to the side. After every Takbīr one should wait as much time as it takes to say سُبْحَانَ الله thrice.

After the third Takbīr, one should fold the hands instead of dropping them. Now the Imām should read Ta'awwuz and Bismillāh, and recite Sūrah Fātiha along with another Sūrah. The Muqtadīs will remain silent as usual.

After reciting the Sūrahs and performing Rukū' and Sujood, the Imām should stand and recite Sūrah Fātiha and another Sūrah in the second Rak'ah. Then, he will say Takbīr thrice as before. However, this time, after the third Takbīr, the hands will not be folded. Rather, they will be dropped to the side, and Rukū' will be performed after saying the fourth Takbīr.

NOTE

When everyone has prayed Eid Salāh, someone who has missed it cannot pray it alone.

If someone missed the first Rak'ah of the prayer with the Imām when he is making up that Rak'ah at the end, he should first recite the Qir'āt and then do the Takbīrs.

If someone joins the Eid Salāh and the Imām has already said the Takbīrs, he should immediately make Niyyah and say the three Takbīrs. If he joins the Salāh when the Imām is in Rukū' and he strongly believes that he has time to say the Takbīrs and then join the Rukū', he should do so. Otherwise, he should go into Rukū' and say the Takbīrs whilst in Rukū'. He will not raise the hands and he won't have to read the usual Tasbīh of Rukū' (سُبْحَانَ رَبِّيَ العَظِيْم). If he was not able to complete the three Takbīrs by the time the Imām rises from Rukū', he too should stand. His remaining Takbīr's are excused.

MASNŪNĀT−E−EID UL FITR [THE SUNNAHS OF EID UL FITR]

[1] Personal elegance and adornment.

[2] Doing Miswaak/cleaning the mouth thoroughly.

[3] Bathing.

[4] Wearing nice clothes.

[5] Applying perfume.

[6] Rising early in the morning.

[7] Going to the Masjid (place of Eid Salāh) early.

[8] Eating something sweet (e.g. dried dates) before going to the Masjid.

[9] Going to the place of Eid Salāh one way and returning a different way.

[10] Going to the place of Eid Salāh on foot.

[11] To softly recite اَللهُ اَكْبَرُ اَللهُ اَكْبَرُ لَا اِلٰهَ اِلَّا اللهُ وَاللهُ اَكْبَرُ اَللهُ اَكْبَرُ وِللهِ الحَمْد whilst going to the place of Eid Salāh.

SADAQAH−E−FITR

It is obligatory (Wājib) for a person to pay Sadaqah-e-Fitr if his property meets the minimum requirement for the imposition of Zakāh (Nisāb), after excluding the essential things, even if he hasn't been in possession of the property for a full year.

On the day of Eid ul Fitr, if one possesses Nisāb, he must pay Sadaqah-e-Fitr. The passing of a whole year is not a condition of Sadaqah-e-Fitr. This is the difference between Zakāh and Sadaqah-e-Fitr.

It is obligatory for a person to pay Sadaqah-e-Fitr for himself and his minor (non Bāligh) children. If the minor children are wealthy, then it is essential to pay from their property and there is no compulsion on the father to pay.

Sadaqah-e-Fitr becomes obligatory at Subhe Sadiq on Eid day. It is therefore not binding on a child born after Subhe Sadiq or a man who dies before Subhe Sadiq.

QUANTITY OF SADAQAH−E−FITR

The required quantity of Sadaqah-e-Fitr is 1.661kg of wheat or wheat flour, but as a precaution one should give more. If one gives barely or barley flour, it should be twice as much as the wheat.

If someone offers some grain other than wheat and barley, then it is according to the price. The price of that grain should match the value of the required quantity of wheat or barley. It would be better just to give the price of wheat or barley.

If someone didn't pay Sadaqah-e-Fitr on Eid day like he was supposed to, it will not be forgiven. It is necessary to pay it afterwards.

THE COMPLETE GUIDE TO FASTING

While writing the above, Shaykh Abdul Raheem (Hafizahullāh) came across the following article written by Sister Naielah Ackbarali and felt it would be beneficial to the reader and so included it here. May Allāh 🌺 reward her. Āmīn.

Fasting the month of Ramadhān is one of the five pillars of Islam. The Companion Abdullāh ibn Umar ibn al-Khattāb (Allāh be pleased with him) said, "I heard the Messenger of Allāh (Allāh bless him and give him peace) say: 'The religion of Islam is based upon five (pillars): testifying that there is no deity except God and Muhammad is the Messenger of God; establishing the prayer; giving zakat; making pilgrimage; and fasting (the month) of Ramadhān.'" [163]

In truth, fasting the month of Ramadhān is one of the greatest acts of worship a believer can perform. It is an act that cleanses one's mind, body, and soul from the spiritual and physical impurities of this world. It is an act that brings the hearts of Muslims together on a worldwide level as they endeavour to practice the virtue of self-discipline in unison. And it is an act that satiates the hungry soul for its eagerness to please the Lord of the Worlds.

Previous religious communities also practiced the act of fasting. Likewise, it has been ordained for the followers of the Prophet Muhammad (Allāh bless him and give him peace). Allāh All-Mighty says in the Qur'ān, "O ye who believe! Fasting is prescribed onto you as it was prescribed onto those before you, that perhaps ye may (learn) self-restraint." [164]

WHAT IS FASTING ?

Linguistically, the word fasting in the Arabic language means unconditional 'restraint' (imsak) from any action or speech during any time.

According to the Sacred Law, fasting is the act of:

---

[163] Bukhārī; Muslim.
[164] Qur'ān 2:183.

[1] Refraining from engaging in sexual activity.

[2] Refraining from entering anything into the body cavity.

[3] Whether deliberately or accidentally.

[4] From the time the sun begins to rise (i.e. the stroke of Dawn, Subhe-Sadiq) to the time the sun sets.

[5] Accompanied with the intention of fasting.

[6] From individuals who are permitted to fast.

'Refraining from engaging in sexual activity' includes actual sexual intercourse and ejaculation caused by foreplay.

'Refraining from entering anything into the body cavity' refers to the acts of entering food, drink, or medicine into the body cavity, regardless of whether this is a typical item one would enter into the body cavity or not. Entering any of these substances inside the body cavity means that the substance enters into the throat, the intestines, the stomach, or the brain by way of the nose, the throat, the private parts, or open wounds.

'Whether deliberately or accidentally' excludes forgetful acts of eating, drinking, or sexual activity.

'From the time the sun begins to rise to the time the sun sets' refers to the true entering of the Fajr time to the entering of the Maghrib time.

'Accompanied with the intention of fasting' means that one must intend to fast in order to distinguish if one is really performing an act of worship or not when one refrains from eating, drinking, or having sexual intercourse. For example, if one were to merely stay away from food, drink, or sexual activity without an intention to fast, then this fast is not valid and does not count.

'From individuals who are permitted to fast' means that one must be free from a situation that would prevent the validity of one's fast, such as menstruation or lochia (post-natal bleeding). [165]

---

[165] Shurunbulali, Maraqi al-Falah; Ala al-Din Abidin, al-Hadiyya al-Alaiyya; Shurunbulali Imdad al-Fattah.

WHEN DOES FASTING BECOME OBLIGATORY?

Fasting the month of Ramadhān is obligatory upon every Muslim, male and female, who is sane and pubescent (Bāligh). This ruling also applies to making up any unperformed Ramadhān fasts whether due to an excuse or one's own remissness. Therefore, a person is obliged to makeup missed Ramadhān fasts. [166]

A male child becomes Bāligh (pubescent), when he experiences a wet dream or ejaculation. A female child becomes pubescent when she experiences a wet dream or her first menstruation. If by the age of 15 lunar years neither male nor female has undergone these experiences, then they are considered legally pubescent and are obliged to fast.

Fasting the current month of Ramadhān is obligatory upon the aforementioned individuals if they are physically able to fast, free from menstruation and lochia (post-natal bleeding), and resident (not a Shar'ee traveller). [167]

WHO IS EXCUSED FROM FASTING THE MONTH OF RAMADHAN?

Fasting the month of Ramadhān is not obligatory upon a menstruating woman or a woman in the state of lochia (post-natal bleeding) because fasting is not permitted while they are in this state. [168]

Sick people and women who are pregnant or breastfeeding are obliged to fast. However, illness can excuse a person from fasting if one reasonably fears that the act of fasting would increase the sickness or slow the recovery process. The same ruling applies to a woman who is pregnant or breastfeeding and reasonably fears that fasting will harm her or her baby. Reasonable fear is known by:

[1] Manifest signs.
[2] A relevant past experience.

---

[166] Shurunbulali, Maraqi al-Falah.
[167] ibid.
[168] Shurunbulali, Imdad al-Fattah.

[3] The notification of an upright, Muslim doctor/expert. [169]

A traveller is also excused from fasting if he initiates his journey before the time of Fajr enters. However, it is better that he fasts providing that this does not cause undue hardship. If a person begins fasting a day of Ramadhān and then travels, he is obliged to complete his fast. [170]

All of the aforementioned individuals are obliged to make up their missed fasts once Ramadhān has ended in a time that they are able. There is no expiation for a person who delays making up their missed fasts, though it is superior to make them up immediately if they are able. [171]

WHAT ARE THE DIFFERENT TYPES OF FASTS?
There are essentially 9 types of fasts:

[1] Specified* Obligatory (fardh) fasts: the current month of Ramadhān (أداء رمضان)

[2] Non-Specified Obligatory (fardh) fasts: make up fasts from a past Ramadhān (قضاء رمضان)

[3] Specified Necessary (Wājib) fasts: specified vowed fasts (نذر معيّن)

[4] Non-Specified Necessary (Wājib) fasts:

　a. Non-specified vowed fasts (نذر مطلق)

　b. Expiation fasts (كفارة)

　c. Make up fasts for any vowed, Sunnah, Nafl, or expiation fast that one vitiated قضاء النذر والسنة والنفل والكفارة

---

169 Shurunbulali, Maraqi al-Falah; Shurunbulali, Imdad al-Fattah
170 ibid.
171 ibid.

[5] Emphasised Sunnah fast (سنة مؤكدة):

    a. The 9th of Dhul al-Hijjah (the day of Arafat)
    b. The 10th of Muharram (the day of 'Ashura) along with either the ninth or the eleventh day.

[6] Recommended fasts (مستحب):

    a. 13th, 14th, 15th days of each lunar month (full moon days)
    b. Every Monday and Thursday of each month.
    c. 6 days of the month of Shawwal; it is best to perform them consecutively. Any other fast established by a request or promise of reward from the Sunnah, like the fast of Dāwūd (fasting every other day), which is said to be the most beloved fast to Allāh.

[7] Voluntary (Nafl نفل) fasts: any fast other than the aforementioned as long as it is not disliked

[8] Slightly Disliked (Makrūh Tanzīhī مكروه تنزيهي) fasts:

    a. Only fasting 10th of Muharram without the ninth or eleventh day, singling out Friday if one specifically thinks that there is reward in it, otherwise there is no dislikedness
    b. Singling out Saturday, though there is no dislikedness if it coincides with another type of fast
    c. Continuously fasting without breaking one's fast in the evening (wisal)

[9] Prohibitively disliked (Makrūh Taḥrīmī مكروه تحريمي) sinful fasts:
    a. the day of Eid al-Fitr

b. the day of Eid al-Adhā and the three days that follow (al-Ayām al-Tashrīq) [172]

*Specified fast means that there is a specific time designated for performing this fast. [173] As such, one is obliged to fast this day, and one cannot intend to fast a different type of fast.

Non-Specified fast means that there is not a specific time designated for performing this fast. Therefore, it is possible to choose when to fast it. The distinction between specified and non-specified also returns to rulings related to the intention, which is forthcoming.

WHAT ARE THE STIPULATIONS FOR A VALID FAST ?

The stipulations for a valid fast are:

[1] the intention
[2] to be free from menstruation and lochia, and
[3] to be free from anything else that would break the fast. [174]

It is not a condition for the validity of the fast that a person be free from the state of major ritual impurity (janāba). The mother of the believers, Ā'isha (Allāh be pleased with her) said, "Fajr would enter during the month of Ramadhān and the Messenger of Allāh (Allāh bless him and give him peace) would be in a state of major ritual purity from other than a sexual dream (i.e. because of sexual relations). He would perform the purificatory bath and fast (that day)." [175]

Likewise, if one intended to fast during the night and woke up within Fajr time in a state of major ritual impurity, then one must perform the

---

[172] [Shurunbulali, Maraqi al-Falah; Ala al-Din Abidin, al-Hadiyya al-Alaiyya; Shurunbulali Imdad al-Fattah; Tahtawi, Hashiyya al-Tahtawi]
[173] Radd al-Muhtar.
[174] Shurunbulali, Nur al-Iydah.
[175] Muslim.

purificatory bath (ghusl) for the sake of the validity of one's prayers, fast this day, and the fast is considered valid. [176]

WHAT IS THE INTENTION ?

The intention is needed for each day one fasts, even in the month of Ramadhān. [177]

The intention is the determination one feels in the heart to do something. [178]

A way to envision this point is if a person was to ask one what they are doing, one would affirm that they are fasting. Practically-speaking, it is nearly impossible to not have the intention in the Hanafī madhhab. One does not have to verbally state the intention, though it is better. [179]

WHEN DOES ONE MAKE THE INTENTION ?

The time of the intention depends on the type of fast.

Category A

For the specified obligatory, specified necessary, emphasised Sunnah, recommended, and nafl fasts, the following rulings apply to the intention:

[1] One must make the intention in the appropriate time in order for the fast to count.

[2] The time of the intention is from Maghrib of the previous night to before the Islamic midday (see definition below) of the following day. This is providing that one did nothing that would invalidate the fast from the start of Fajr time.

---

[176] Shurunbulali, Maraqi al-Falah; Shurunbulali, Imdad al-Fattah.
[177] Shurunbulali, Imdad al-Fattah; Ala al-Din Abidin, al-Hadiyya al-Alaiyya.
[178] Ala al-Din Abidin, al-Hadiyya al-Alaiyya.
[179] ibid.

[3] Scholars confirm that it is superior for one to make the intention the night before one fasts (i.e. any time from Maghrib to the entering of Fajr) due to the difference of opinion from other schools on this point.

[4] It is sufficient to intend to fast without specifying if the fast is obligatory, necessary, Sunnah, recommended, or nafl. [180]

Category B

For non-specified obligatory and non-specified necessary fasts, the following rulings apply to the intention:

[1] One must make the intention in the appropriate time in order for the fast to count.

[2] The time for the intention is from Maghrib of the previous night to the entering of Fajr on the day one desires to fast.

[3] One must also specify the type of fast when intending.

[4] If one made the intention after the entering of Fajr to before the Islamic midday (see definition below), then this fast counts as a voluntary (nafl) fast instead. [181]

WHEN IS THE ISLAMIC MIDDAY?

The Islamic midday (al-Dahwa al-Kubra) is the half-way point between the entering of Fajr time to the entering of Maghrib time. It does not mean noon, nor does it mean the Zawāl. [182]

For example, if Fajr entered at 5am and Maghrib entered at 5pm, then the Islamic midday would be the halfway point between this 12-hour time span,

---

[180] Shurunbulali, Imdad al-Fattah; Ala al-Din Abidin, al-Hadiyya al-Alaiyya; al-Fatāwā al-Hindiyyah.

[181] Shurunbulali, Imdad al-Fattah; Ala al-Din Abidin, al-Hadiyya al-Alaiyya.

[182] Mulla Khusru, Durar al-Hikam Sharh Ghurar al-Ahkam; ibn Abidin, Radd al-Muhtar.

which is 11am. Thus, in this example, a person would have from the entering of Maghrib of the previous night to before 11am of the next day to make the intention if he is performing a fast from category A.

The intention must be made 'before' the Islamic midday because one needs to fast with the intention for the majority of the day.

According to the Sacred Law, this would be similar to fasting the entire day. [183]

WHAT HAPPENS IF ONE DECIDES NOT TO FAST?

It is a condition that the intention to fast remains with one. If during the night one decides to not fast the next day after previously intending to fast it, then one is not considered to be fasting for that day. If one renewed the intention, however, then one is considered to be fasting. [184]

WHAT ARE SOME RECOMMENDED ACTS WHILE FASTING?

[1] To eat the pre-dawn meal (suhoor) before Fajr time enters.

[2] To delay the pre-dawn meal closer to the time before Fajr enters.

[3] To hasten to break one's fast at the entering of Maghrib. [185]

WHAT ARE SOME DUĀS TO READ WHEN BREAKING THE FAST?

Allāhumma laka sumtu wa bika aamantu wa 'alayka tawakkaltu wa 'ala rizqika aftartu wa sawm al-ghad min shahr Ramadhān nawaytu faghfir li ma qaddamtu wa ma akh-khartu

---

[183] Mulla Khusru, Durar al-Hikam Sharh Ghurar al-Ahkam; ibn Abidin, Radd al-Muhtar.
[184] Shurunbulali, Imdad al-Fattah; Ala al-Din Abidin, al-Hadiyya al-Alaiyya.
[185] Shurunbulali, Nur al-Iydah.

Translation: "Oh Allāh, for You I fasted, and in You I believe, and on You I place my reliance, and on Your provision I break my fast. And I intend the fasting of tomorrow for the month of Ramadhān. Forgive me for what I did before and what I do after."

Allāhumma laka sumtu wa 'ala rizqika aftartu

Translation: "Oh Allāh for You I fasted and upon Your provision I break my fast."

Allāhumma laka sumna wa 'ala rizqika aftarna fataqabbal minna innaka Anta al-Sami' al-'Alim.

Translation: "Oh Allāh for You we fasted, and upon Your provision we break our fasts. Accept this from us. Verily, You are All-Hearing, All-Knowing." [186]

WHAT DOES A WOMAN DO IF HER PERIOD STARTS IN RAMADHĀN?

If her menstruation starts in Ramadhān during the night (i.e. any time from the entering of Maghrib to before the entering of Fajr), then she refrains from fasting the following day and for the duration that she is menstruating. [187]

If her menstruation starts in Ramadhān during the day (i.e. any time from the entering of Fajr to the entering of Maghrib), then her fast is vitiated and it does not count. She must make up this day after Ramadhān has ended in a time when she is able. She must refrain from fasting for the duration that she is menstruating. [188]

A menstruating woman can eat and drink during the day in Ramadhān. If she believes that it is unlawful for her to eat or drink, then it is necessary for

---

[186] Nawawi, al-Adhkar; Tahtawi, Hashiyya al-Tahtawi.

[187] Hidāyah Hartford, Birgivi's Manual Interpreted.

[188] Shurunbulali, Maraqi al-Falah; Shurunbulali, Imdad al-Fattah; Tahtawi, Hashiyya al-Tahtawi.

her to do so as refraining from food or drink with the intention of fasting is unlawful for her. [189]

A menstruating woman should record the number of days she missed while fasting and make them up after Ramadhān ends in a time when she is able. The same rulings apply to a woman in a state of lochia (post-natal bleeding).

WHAT DOES A WOMAN DO IF HER PERIOD ENDS IN RAMADHĀN ?

If her menstruation stops in Ramadhān during the night (i.e. any time from the entering of Maghrib to before the entering of Fajr), then she performs a purificatory bath (ghusl), begins her obligatory worship, and she is obliged to fast the following day and the remainder of Ramadhān. [190]

Note: There are details to this point if her menstruation ends before the menstrual maximum of 10 complete days and the ghusl time finishes within the Fajr time. Please refer to Hidāyah Hartford's 'Birgivi's Manual Interpreted.'

If her menstruation stops in Ramadhān during the day (i.e. any time after the entering of Fajr up to the entering of Maghrib), then she performs a purificatory bath (ghusl), begins her obligatory worship and she acts like a fasting person until the Maghrib time enters due to the sacredness of the month of Ramadhān. [191]

It is necessary for her to abstain from eating and drinking for the remainder of the day. [192]

She is sinful if she does not do so. However, this day of acting like a fasting person does not count as a fast. She must make up this day after Ramadhān has ended in a time when she is able. [193]

She is obliged to fast the following day and the remainder of Ramadhān.

A menstruating woman should record the number of days she missed while fasting and make them up after Ramadhān ends in a time when she is able.

---

[189] Tahtawi, Hashiyya al-Tahtawi; Shurunbulali, Imdad al-Fattah.

[190] Hidāyah Hartford, Birgivi's Manual Interpreted.

[191] Hidayah Hartford, Birgivi's Manual Interpreted.

[192] Shurunbulali, Maraqi al-Falah; Shurunbulali, Imdad al-Fattah.

[193] Ibid.

The same rulings apply to a woman in a state of lochia (post-natal bleeding).

ARE THERE ACTIONS THAT CAN VITIATE THE FAST?

Yes, there are actions that can vitiate the fast. These actions fall under two categories:

[1] That which vitiates the fast and requires a makeup along with expiation.
[2] That which vitiates the fast and requires makeup only. [194]

For the first category, the principle returns to deliberately performing an act that vitiates the fast by one's own free will and without a valid reason. Deliberately means that one remembers that one is fasting and purposely performs an action that breaks the fast. [195]

These actions are outlined below in the section 'category 1.'

For the second category, the principle returns to accidentally performing an act that vitiates the fast. It also includes acts performed by force of a third party. Accidentally means that one remembers that one is fasting but broke the fast by one's own doing without the intention to purposely break the fast. [196]

These actions are outlined below in the section 'category 2.'

If any of the actions from category 1 are performed forgetfully, then they do not vitiate the fast. Forgetfully means that one does not have the presence of mind that one is fasting when performing the action. [197]

The Prophet (Allāh bless him and give him peace) said, "Whoever forgets that he is fasting and eats or drinks, then he still completes his fast. It is only Allāh who fed him and gave him drink." [198]

---

[194] ibn Abdin, Radd al-Muhtar.
[195] Ibid.
[196] Tahtawi, Hashiyya al-Tahtawi; Related in Radd al-Muhtar.
[197] Shurunbulali, Imdad al-Fattah.
[198] Bukhārī.

In another narration, the Prophet (Allāh bless him and give him peace) said, "If a fasting person eats forgetfully, it is only provision Allāh put forth to him and there is no makeup upon him." [199]

CATEGORY 1 : ACTS THAT VITIATE THE FAST AND REQUIRE MAKEUP AND EXPIATION

Acts that invalidate the fast and require a makeup along with expiation only relate to the current Ramadhān fasts. Otherwise, if one performs any of the following actions while performing a fast outside of the current month of Ramadhān, such as a make-up fast, then the fast is vitiated and only a makeup is required. One does not owe the expiation.

If done deliberately, by one's own free will, and without a valid reason while fasting a current Ramadhān fast, the following acts invalidate the fast and require a makeup along with expiation:

[1] Eating or drinking something that humans would normally consume and this consummation nourishes, medicates, or pleases the body in some way.

[2] Actual sexual intercourse, in the front or rear private part*, regardless if one ejaculated or not.

[3] Swallowing the saliva of one's spouse. [200]

*It is impermissible and a grave crime to engage in sexual intercourse from the rear private part. The Sacred Law unconditionally prohibits this type of sexual activity whether during or not during the month of Ramadhān.

WHAT IS THE EXPIATION ?

The expiation is to fast sixty consecutive days in the year without any interruption. One must choose a time where one can fast these sixty days

---

[199] Bukhārī.
[200] Shurunbulali, Maraqi al-Falah; Ala al-Din Abidin, al-Hadiyya al-Alaiyya.

without the days of Eid or the three days after Eid al-Adhā (al-Ayyam al-Tashrīq) interrupting the fasts because of the prohibition of fasting on these days. [201]

If one does not fast them consecutively, then one must restart the 60-day period each time the continuity of the fasts is broken. [202]

The only exceptions to this rule are if one is menstruating or in a state of lochia (post-natal bleeding). A menstruating woman must continue to fast after she becomes pure, and she cannot delay the completion of the expiation. If she does delay fasting after becoming pure, then she must restart the 60 days of fasting. [203]

The same ruling applies to a woman in the state of lochia.

If one is genuinely unable to perform the sixty consecutive fasts based on reasonable surety, then one must either:

[1] Feed the same sixty, poor people to their fill for two meals.

[2] Feed one poor person to his fill for two meals a day for sixty days.

[3] Give sixty poor people half a sa' [204] of wheat (or similar food grains) or its monetary value.

[4] Sixty poor people a sa'* of dates (or similar food grains) or its monetary value.

[5] Give one poor person either 3 or 4 for sixty days. It is important to note that one does not have a choice between fasting sixty days and feeding sixty poor people. Rather, one is obliged to fast sixty days, unless one is genuinely unable to perform all of these fasts based on reasonable surety.

Reasonable surety is known by:

---

[201] Shurunbulali, Maraqi al-Falah.
[202] Tahtawi, Hashiyya al-Tahtawi.
[203] Tahtawi, Hashiyya al-Tahtawi.
[204] Half a sa' is approximately 2 kilos (4.5 pounds). A full sa' is approximately 4 kilos (9 pounds).

[1] Manifest signs.

[2] A relevant past experience.

[3] The notification of an upright, Muslim doctor/expert.

One expiation suffices for all previous violations performed, even if they occurred in separate Ramadhān's. However, if one performed a future violation after the performance of the expiation, then a new expiation is owed. [205]

CATEGORY 2 : ACTS THAT VITIATE THE FAST AND REQUIRE MAKE UP BUT DO NOT REQUIRE EXPIATION

This category includes any act that vitiates the fast if done accidentally (see aforementioned definition) or by force of another.

It also includes any makeup fast one vitiated while trying to make it up.

THE MOUTH AND THROAT

- Eating or drinking accidentally
- Eating or drinking because one thought Maghrib entered but Maghrib did not enter
- Eating or drinking because one doubted that Fajr entered but Fajr really did enter
- Eating or drinking forgetfully and thereafter thinking that the fast is broken, to deliberately eat and drink again
- Swallowing what is between the teeth, on the condition that it is the size of a chickpea or bigger
- Swallowing a pebble or other items that people wouldn't typically eat

---

[205] Shurunbulali, Maraqi al-Falah; Ala al-Din Abidin, al-Hadiyya al-Alaiyya; Shurunbulali Imdad al-Fattah.

- Swallowing water by accident when gargling for Wudhū or ghusl (with the exception of water that remains in the mouth—see next category)
- Swallowing blood that exits from the gums and preponderates over the saliva
- Swallowing toothpaste or mouthwash
- Deliberately swallowing vomit that reaches a mouthful
- Deliberately vomiting a mouthful, regardless if one swallows it or not
- Vomiting and thereafter thinking that the fast is broken, to deliberately vomit again
- Smoke that enters the throat by one's doing (on the condition one's body doesn't benefit from it).
- Kissing that causes one to ejaculate (on the condition one did not swallow the other's saliva).

THE PRIVATE PARTS

- Engaging in sexual intercourse because one still thinks Fajr has not entered but it really has
- Engaging in sexual intercourse forgetfully and thereafter thinking that the fast is broken, to deliberately have sexual intercourse again
- Entering a suppository into the anus
- Entering something dry into the anus and it completely disappears inside the body
- Entering something wet or oiled into the anus, even if it does not completely disappear inside of the body
- Entering a wet tissue or a wet piece of cotton into the vagina, even if it does not completely disappear inside of the body
- Entering a dry tissue or a dry piece of cotton into the vagina and it is completely inserted inside of the body without any part remaining outside

- Pouring water or oil into the anus and it reaches the distance of the mihqana [206]
- Pouring water or oil into the vagina and it reaches the distance of the mihqana

THE NOSE

- Water used to clean the nose for Wudhū or ghusl reaches the throat or the brain
- Inhaling medicine into the nostrils
- Inhaling smoke by one's doing (on the condition one's body doesn't benefit from it)

THE BODY, IN GENERAL

- Touching that causes one to ejaculate (this includes masturbation)
- Applying medicine to an open abdominal or head wound and it reaches the stomach or the brain [207]

WHAT ARE THE ACTS THAT DO NOT BREAK THE FAST?

THE MOUTH AND THROAT

- Eating or drinking something forgetfully (see aforementioned definition)

---

[206] The mihqana, or huqna in other relations, is a device used to insert medicine into the body by way of the anus (medical term: enema). In our day, a mihqana is similar to a rectal syringe or a clyster-pipe. The distance that breaks the fast is determined by when the top of mihqana reaches the place where medicine is released from it to the intestines. [Radd al-Muhtar]

[207] Shurunbulali, Maraqi al-Falah; Ala al-Din Abidin, al-Hadiyya al-Alaiyya; Shurunbulali Imdad al-Fattah.

- Eating what is between the teeth if it is less than the size of a chickpea
- Tasting the leftover traces of medicine in the mouth or throat
- Chewing on a sesame seed without swallowing it, if its taste doesn't reach the throat
- Dust or smoke (including smoke from 'ud or incense) entering one's throat without one's doing
- A mosquito, fly, or any other object entering one's throat without one's doing
- Swallowing the wetness that remains after washing one's mouth for Wudhū or ghusl
- Swallowing one or two drops of sweat or tears that enter the mouth and mixes with one's saliva, on the condition that one cannot taste its saltiness
- Swallowing one's own saliva
- Swallowing one's own phlegm after clearing the throat
- Swallowing vomit that emerges in the mouth without one's doing, even if it is a mouthful
- Deliberately vomiting less than a mouthful, regardless if one swallows it or not
- Using a Miswaak or toothbrush (without toothpaste)
- Wetting one's lips with one's saliva while speaking and swallowing it
- Swallowing blood that exits from the gums and does not preponderate over the saliva on the condition one cannot taste it
- Pulling back saliva into one's mouth that flows to the chin like a string on the condition that it stays connected and does not break off. (If one takes saliva in the hand and then swallows it, it will break the fast.
- Backbiting

THE PRIVATE PARTS

- Performing sexual intercourse forgetfully

- The state of major ritual impurity (janāba) suddenly befalls one, such as from a wet dream
- Ejaculation caused by looking or thinking
- Entering a dry finger into the anus
- Pouring water or oil into the male urethra
- Entering tissue or a piece of cotton into the male urethra, even if it completely disappears inside the body
- Entering a dry finger into the vagina
- Entering a dry tissue or a dry piece of cotton into the vagina upon the condition that part of it remains outside of the body
- Performing istinjā with water, providing that the wetness doesn't reach the distance of the mihqana (see aforementioned definition)

THE NOSE

- Mucus descending from the nose
- Sniffing up mucus that is in the nose and it descends to one's throat
- Inhaling smoke, perfume, or incense without one's doing
- Smelling an odour

THE EYES

- Applying kuhl in the eyes, even if one finds its taste in the throat or its colour in the saliva or phlegm
- Dripping eye drops or contact solution into the eyes
- Wearing contact lenses

THE EARS

- Water entering the ears from a bath
- Scratching the inside of one's ear with a q-tip, even if dirt exits and one reinserts it into the ear

114

THE BODY, IN GENERAL

- Rubbing oil or cream on the body or hair
- Applying deodorant
- Performing a bath and finding its coolness penetrating into one's body
- Withdrawing blood, such as in a blood test
- Blood cupping

THE MIND

- Intending to break one's fast but not actually doing it [208]

WHAT ARE THE ACTS THAT ARE DISLIKED WHILE FASTING (مكروهات)?

- Tasting or chewing something without an excuse, provided that its flavour is not swallowed
- Chewing flavourless gum
- Kissing with desire in which one fears falling into sexual intercourse or ejaculation, on the condition one did not swallow the other's saliva
- Gathering saliva in the mouth and then swallowing it
- To gargle excessively when making Wudhū or ghusl for fear of breaking the fast
- To sniff water excessively when cleaning the nose in Wudhū or ghusl for fear of breaking the fast
- Doing things that would weaken one while fasting, like cupping or withdrawing blood

---

[208] Shurunbulali, Maraqi al-Falah; Ala al-Din Abidin, al-Hadiyya al-Alaiyya; Shurunbulali Imdad al-Fattah.

- Brushing the teeth with toothpaste or using mouthwash, on the condition one does not swallow it [209]

CAN I BE AFFECTIONATE WITH MY SPOUSE WHILE FASTING ?

There are different rulings related to this question due to the various ways one can be affectionate.

PHYSICAL CONTACT THAT DOES NOT VITIATE THE FAST

- Non-passionate kissing in which one is free from swallowing the saliva of one's spouse and free from the fear of falling into sexual intercourse or ejaculation
- Non-passionate touching in which one is free from the fear of falling into sexual intercourse or ejaculation, such as hugging or holding hands
- Looking at one's spouse, even if one ejaculates

PHYSICAL CONTACT THAT DOES NOT VITIATE THE FAST BUT IS PROHIBITIVELY DISLIKED & SINFUL

- Kissing with desire in which one fears falling into sexual intercourse or ejaculation
- Touching with desire in which one fears falling into sexual intercourse or ejaculation
- Anything sexual that one fears will lead to sexual intercourse or ejaculation

---

[209] Shurunbulali, Maraqi al-Falah; Ala al-Din Abidin, al-Hadiyya al-Alaiyya; Shurunbulali Imdad al-Fattah.

PHYSICAL CONTACT THAT VITIATES THE FAST AND REQUIRES MAKEUP ONLY

- Ejaculation from masturbation*
- Kissing and touching (i.e. no actual penetration took place) that causes ejaculation*

PHYSICAL CONTACT THAT VITIATES THE FAST AND REQUIRES MAKEUP AND EXPIATION**

- Deliberate passionate kissing that causes one to swallow the saliva of one's spouse*
- Deliberate sexual intercourse in one of the private parts with ejaculation*
- Deliberate sexual intercourse in one of the private parts without ejaculation*

*The person who involved himself in the above-mentioned situations should refrain from eating, drinking, and sexual activity for the remainder of that day, as well as repenting for the severity of the sin.

**Outside the month of Ramadhān, if one breaks a fast deliberately through these acts, then the expiation is not required. [210]

WHAT IS THE I'TIKĀF [SPIRITUAL RETREAT] ?

The mother of the believers, Ā'ishā (Allāh be pleased with her) said, "The Prophet (Allāh bless him and give him peace) would always perform I'tikāf in the last ten days of Ramadhān until Allāh Most High took his soul (Allāh bless him and give him peace)." [211]

---

[210] Shurunbulali, Maraqi al-Falah; Ala al-Din Abidin, al-Hadiyya al-Alaiyya.
[211] Bukhārī.

The scholar al-Zahidi said, "It is strange how the people have left performing the I'tikāf. The Messenger of Allāh (Allāh bless him and give him peace) performed some actions and left them, but he never left the I'tikāf – from the time he entered Madina to the moment he died (Allāh bless him and give him peace)."

The I'tikāf is entering the masjid with the intention to remain there for worship. The masjid must be one where the group prayer is offered for the five obligatory prayers.

The I'tikāf is permissible if one is free from a state of major ritual impurity, menstruation, and lochia (post-natal bleeding).

The conditions for a valid vowed I'tikāf (see definition below) are:

[1] The intention
[2] To be Muslim
[3] Sanity
[4] To be free from menstruation and lochia (post-natal bleeding) [212]

WHAT ARE THE TYPES OF I'TIKĀF?

NECESSARY [WĀJIB]: THE VOWED I'TIKĀF

The vowed I'tikāf is an oath to make i`tikāf for a specified time. It must be at least an entire day and night. One is obliged to fast during it in order for the vowed I'tikāf to count.

EMPHASISED SUNNAH: THE LAST TEN DAYS AND NIGHTS OF RAMADHĀN

Performing I'tikāf in the last ten days and nights of Ramadhān is a strongly emphasised communal Sunnah. It is blameworthy upon the community, as a whole to not perform the I'tikāf. If some people perform the I'tikāf and others do not, then they raise the blameworthiness from the entire community.

---

[212] Ala al-Din Abidin, al-Hadiyya al-Alaiyya.

The scholars do not stipulate that one must fast during the emphasised Sunnah I'tikāf because it is performed during Ramadhān and the assumption is that the person will be fasting anyway.

RECOMMENDED: ANY TIMES OTHER THAN THE AFOREMENTIONED

For the recommended I'tikāf, its minimum duration is a moment, even if it's when one passes through the mosque. Fasting is not a condition for the commended I'tikāf. [213]

CAN A WOMAN PERFORM I'TIKĀF?

Yes, a woman can perform I'tikāf.

- A woman's I'tikāf is best performed in the prayer area of her house.
- The prayer area is the place where she has designated to pray her obligatory and nafl prayers.
- It is disliked for a woman to perform I'tikāf in the masjid.
- It is not valid for men to perform I'tikāf in other than the masjid. [214]

CAN ONE LEAVE THE MASJID DURING I'TIKĀF?

Leaving the masjid without an excuse ends the I'tikāf. This ruling also applies to a woman performing I'tikāf in the prayer area of her house. If one does leave because of an excuse, the excuse must be due to a Sharī'ah-compliant need, or to use the restroom if unable to use the masjid facilities, or out of necessity. [215]

---

[213] Shurunbulali, Maraqi al-Falah; Ala al-Din Abidin, al-Hadiyya al-Alaiyya.
[214] Ala al-Din Abidin, al-Hadiyya al-Alaiyya.
[215] Shurunbulali, Imdad al-Fattah.

WHAT DOES A PERSON DO DURING I'TIKAF?

One is encouraged to busy oneself with worship and anything beneficial, such as praying, reciting the Qur'ān, making much dhikr, speaking of the good, and gaining beneficial knowledge.

A person performing I'tikāf can eat, drink, sleep, talk, and do everything that is normally permissible, except for sexual intercourse, kissing, and touching with desire. [216]

Allāh Most High says: "And do not approach your women while you are performing the spiritual retreat in the masjids." [217]

Engaging in these acts end the I'tikāf whether inside or outside of the masjid. For example, if one left the masjid for a Sharī'ah-compliant need and fell into sexual intercourse with one's spouse, then this act ends the I'tikāf. Engaging in these actions end the I'tikāf, regardless of whether one did them during the day or the night. [218]

During the I'tikāf, it is disliked to believe that remaining silent is a form of worship. It is also disliked to engage in work or trade. [219]

May Allāh accept our fasts and any act of worship that we perform for His sake.

---

[216] Shurunbulali, Nur al-Iydah.

[217] Qur'ān 2:187.

[218] Shurunbulali, Maraqi al-Falah; Tahtawi, Hashiyya al-Tahtawi; Shurunbulali Imdad al-Fattah.

[219] Shurunbulali, Nur al-Iydah.